Paper Crafting With Photos™

Edited by Vicki Blizzard

Annie's
Attic®

We all have envelopes and

boxes of extra photographs sitting around waiting for us to take them out and look at them.

After you've scrapbooked everything you possibly can, what do you do with the leftover pictures? We have the answer for you in the pages of this book.

Use a photo of your children to create a fun card to mail to their grandparents or out-of-town relatives. Or use your extra vacation photos to create a unique altered CD that can hang on the wall as a reminder of a summer well spent. We even show you how to use blurry, out-of-focus "dud" photos to create unique woven-look projects. Photos of favorite flowers become bookmarks for gardening books. Well, you get the picture!

Choose a project, find a photo, and get started creating fun and interesting projects!

Warm regards,

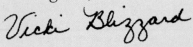

Vicki Blizzard

CONTENTS

Staff
Editor: Vicki Blizzard
Associate Editor: Lisa M. Fosnaugh
Copy Supervisor: Michelle Beck
Copy Editors: Conor Allen, Mary Martin
Technical Editor: Brooke Smith
Graphic Arts Supervisor: Ronda Bechinski
Graphic Artist: Pam Gregory
Photography: Carl Clark
Photo Stylist: Tammy Nussbaum

Paper Crating With Photos is published by Annie's Attic, 306 East Parr Road, Berne, IN 46711, telephone (260) 589-4000. Printed in USA. Copyright © 2005 Annie's Attic. RETAILERS: If you would like to carry this pattern book or any other Annie's Attic publications, call the Wholesale Department at Annie's Attic to set up a direct account: (903) 636-4303. Toll-free order line or to request a free catalog (800) LV-ANNIE (800-582-6643). Customer Service: (800) AT-ANNIE (800-282-6643), Fax (800) 882-6643. Also, request a complete listing of publications available from Annie's Attic. Visit www.AnniesAttic.com.

Every effort has been made to ensure that the instructions in this pattern book are complete and accurate. We cannot, however, take responsibility for human error, typographical mistakes or variations in individual work.

ISBN: 1-59635-012-1
Library of Congress: 2004116367

1 2 3 4 5 6 7 8 9

Crafting With Photos

By MARIA NERIUS

Introduction

If a picture is worth a thousand words, then the projects you can create with your photos are priceless! Don't leave your pictures in a shoebox or put them on a shelf to sort through someday. Use those wonderful photographs to create something grand.

You can have fun with photo transferring, organizing a photo mosaic, colorizing a black-and-white photo to capture the romance of years gone by, and even creating an interesting collage to celebrate your life. The power of the visual medium of photography is made extra special when you add the spirit of creativity. Get out those photos and start a project that will be enjoyed by everyone!

Handy Tools

The list of photo-crafting tools could go on forever, but there are a few that are vital for any project. The first is a sharp cutting tool, which can be traditional scissors, a personal trimmer or a craft knife. It is important that you always work with tools that are sharp. A dull cutting blade or pair of scissors can tear or mar a photo—especially photos that are printed on home printers. These are very functional tools and a must for photo crafting.

Cutting tools can also be just plain fun! There are dozens of decorative scissors, hand paper punches and die-cutting plates to help you create

interesting, exciting edges and corners for your photos. You can choose from deckled edges to postage-stamp edges to traditional zigzag edges to add variety to your projects. Paper punches come in every size and shape from apples to zebras! Dies can usually be found at craft or scrapbook stores where you pay per cut of the die. Dies are available in even more shapes and sizes than hand punches.

Adhesives are important to any craft project. It's best to coordinate the adhesive to the materials you are using. Photos can be attached in a variety of ways, from liquid glue to any of the

many types of tape that are available. If you are adhering anything heavy or nonporous to your photo project, you'll need to consider a specialty paper glue or a jewelry glue, both of which are designed to hold heavier items to a surface. Many artists and crafters are incorporating metal and glass into their photo crafts, and this technique calls for a stronger glue. If you are only working with lightweight embellishments and paper, then most white glues will do the trick. Archival, heirloom and scrapbooking projects

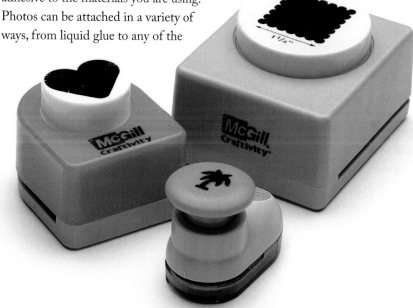

dozens of free stencils and templates to choose from. You can cut an interesting shape, emboss a raised image and fold a beautiful flower all with the help of these tools.

Just a Reminder

You probably have a few older photographs in your collection. It is important to remember that if the photo doesn't have a negative, you might want to craft with a copy of that photo, not the original. Old photos with charming sepia tones or hand tinting are great to craft with, but often are one-of-a-kind family mementoes. Keep the original photograph intact and make a few copies to craft with.

Digital or the Old-Fashioned Way?

It doesn't really matter anymore if you use photos taken with film or photos printed at home from your digital camera. The key is getting the best quality print you can. If you are working with an actual photograph rather than a photocopied print, you need quality photo paper and a quality printer. Photo paper is easy to find for home printers, but home printer quality still doesn't quite match that of a commercial photo developer. You

should use a glue labeled as acid-free to prevent eventual deterioration of the photographs.

Pens, inks, colored or watercolor pencils, markers, chalk and paint all add color and interest to photo crafts. Feel free to use them with splash and flash; however, if creating an archival or heirloom design, keep in mind that there are acid-free pens, colored pencils, inks, markers and paint available. Most of these supplies are indeed acid-free, but not all manufacturers go through the testing process. Call the manufacturer if you have archival quality questions. The same goes for most printer inks; most are acid-free, but are not always labeled as such.

Other handy tools include stencils and templates. These help aid in creating interesting shapes, dimension and folds to your photo craft projects. A huge variety of clever and inspiring stencils and templates are available at art and craft supply stores, and a quick search on the Internet will provide

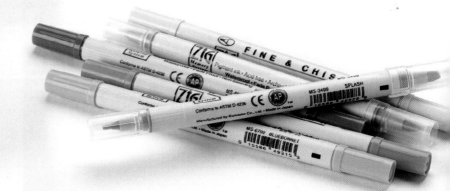

need to decide what you prefer for each individual project you undertake. Sometimes a photo print from your home computer system is fine, while there may be other projects for which you'll prefer to have a professionally printed photo.

Tips for Photographs

To create great photo craft projects, you need to start with great photos! Here are some tips that leading professional photographers pass along to camera enthusiasts.

1 Know your camera. Read your camera manual and refer to it if you have any problems. It is very important you know what all the buttons do and what features are available. Most are there for a good reason and to give you the best possible photos. The next step is to practice and keep your camera handy for any photo opportunity.

2 Do more than just aim and click your camera. Take charge and get the photo you want. As you look through the viewfinder, take time to really see what you are looking at. Ask

people to move closer together for a better shot. Tell Grandpa Ralph to lean slightly to the left or right. Add a prop. Remove a hat. Do whatever it takes to make the photo better, tell a story or make you smile.

3 The most vital part of every photograph you take is light. Lighting affects the appearance of everything you photograph. Harsh light can make your subjects squint and grimace. Not enough light results in shadowy darkness. If the lighting is not right then move yourself or your subject. Check the settings on your camera and adjust for bright light, cloudiness, incandescent or florescent light, and moonlight.

Learn when to use your flash to fill in with supplemental light and when you should use the red-eye reducer. According to a leading camera

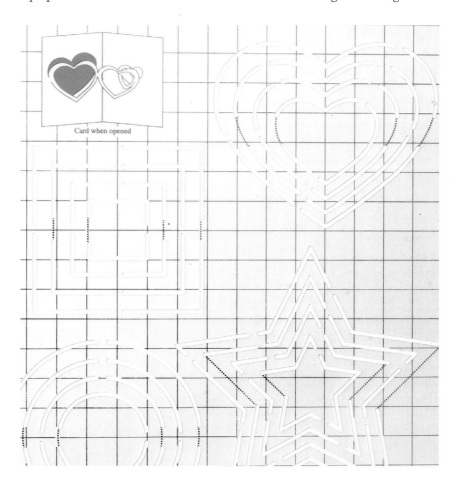

Card when opened

manufacturer, the No. 1 flash mistake is taking pictures beyond the range of the flash. Photos taken beyond the maximum flash range will be too dark. As a general rule most cameras have a maximum flash range of less than 15 feet. You can find the flash range in the camera manual.

4 Get down (or up) to the photo subject's eye level. This is especially important when photographing children and pets. You may have to kneel, bend, hunch or stand on a stool, but the effort is worth it. Being at eye level gives a warm, personal feel to the photo without the necessity of the subject looking directly at the camera lens. In fact, some of the most intimate photos are with the subject looking off to either side of the camera lens.

5 When you look through the camera viewfinder, it is natural for you to focus all of your attention on the subject. However, your camera is not doing the same.

Standing too far away can lead to your subject getting lost in the landscape or background. Move closer so you can see more detail. Or, if your camera has a zoom lens, let the camera do the work by zooming closer. Next time you take a picture of your best friend, let her face fill the viewfinder and you'll get some amazing results.

6 Hold the camera steady with both hands and gently push the shutter button down. Nothing can blur a great photo faster than unsteady hands. Consider using a tripod for posed shots.

7 Most photos are taken with a horizontal frame. It's natural and done without thinking. Why not shoot a photo vertically every now and then? Many things look better when a vertical picture is taken, such as friends standing around a birthday cake, or tall buildings. This adds variety to the photos by showing different lines, shapes, forms and perspective. Next time you get ready to shoot a photo, take a few extra seconds and turn your

camera sideways. You might get a better shot.

8 A plain background gives focus to the subject you are photographing. When you look through the camera viewfinder, learn to pay attention to the area surrounding your subject. Make sure no trees grow from the head of your grandson or no wires seem to be stretching from the sides of Aunt Barb. Keep your photo backgrounds free from clutter.

9 To avoid the dreaded bullseye syndrome, remember the rule of thirds. Divide your photo frame into nine equal segments. Instead of having the focus of your photo in the center of the nine squares, place

Did You Know?

• *People immediately look at another human in a photo* even if the person is very small in the frame. Our attention will go to anything *alive* as opposed to something inanimate. The hierarchy of attention is humans over animals, animals over plants.

• *Colors draw our attention* and the warm shades of red, yellow and orange will jump out of a background of cool-tone colors like blue and green. Even a small subject will dominate if it's different from its surroundings. It could be its color, brightness or the direction it's facing. Anything that's isolated from everything else will draw attention to itself.

• *No matter what else* is in the scene, the eye is irresistibly drawn to the lightest, brightest area. That's why any bright blob of light or bit of paper in the background is distracting. All other things being equal, the eye will go to the area of highest contrast. The eye will go to the subject that's in sharpest focus.

• *Can you crop Polaroid photographs?* Yes and no! Cutting an older Polaroid photograph releases harmful chemicals from inside the image. As an alternative, you can place a frame made of acid-free paper over the top of the photograph, hiding the white borders. According to the manufacturer, photos made from film manufactured after 2003 can be cut without problems.

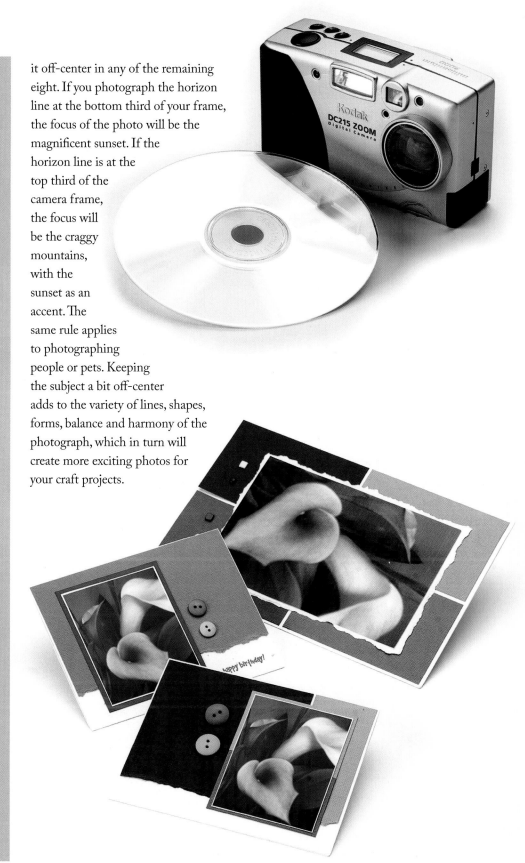

it off-center in any of the remaining eight. If you photograph the horizon line at the bottom third of your frame, the focus of the photo will be the magnificent sunset. If the horizon line is at the top third of the camera frame, the focus will be the craggy mountains, with the sunset as an accent. The same rule applies to photographing people or pets. Keeping the subject a bit off-center adds to the variety of lines, shapes, forms, balance and harmony of the photograph, which in turn will create more exciting photos for your craft projects.

10 Black-and-white photos are known to have a longer life than most color photographs and are often more dramatic, so include black-and-white film in your picture taking. Some digital cameras have a black-and-white (grayscale) mode. You also have an opportunity to include black-and-white style when you scan a photo by using photo-editing software that includes a grayscale feature.

Adding Color to a Black-and-White Photo

Coloring a black-and-white photo can add a special tint to your photo crafts. It is not as hard as you might imagine it to be. The finished effect is nostalgic and romantic. You may find some original hand-colored photos among your older treasured family photos. These photos were probably hand colored by professional photographers using oil paints. This technique is still used and oil paint products are available at art, craft and photography shops. However, modern products have taken much of the tediousness and mystery out of this technique. You no longer have to be a professional artist or even have any artistic ability to hand color photos.

The first rule to remember is never hand color an original black-and-white photo. Have a copy made on photo paper. Remember that any negative can be developed into a black-and-white photo, and a color photo can be printed in black and white at a photo developer or by using your computer. That's right, even your color negatives can be processed into black and white photos. Once the film has been developed, just ask your developer to make some copies in black-and-white. Most shops will not be able to do this process in-house, but it is well worth the extra day or two it takes to obtain black-and-white prints to hand color.

There are three basic methods to hand color an actual photo. The first involves an oil paint as previously

described. This method takes some practice and the paint is applied by brush or paint pen. The second method uses acrylic paint or tints and is applied in the same manner. The final method, and by far the easiest, is to use markers specifically developed to hand color black-and-white photos. Depending on what brand of products are used, you may have to sponge a solution on the photo to soften the top layer, making it more receptive to color. You'll then apply the color. You may have to use an aerosol finish on the photo once completed to preserve the color.

Photo-coloring markers provide very transparent tinting. Add color in a circular motion, and apply layer upon layer of color until the desired intensity is reached. Experiment with different colors. Many manufacturers carry stock colors that are close to the original hues used by professionals in days of old. Many manufacturers also include modern colors in their palettes.

You can also use colored pencils to add soft color to photos. Photocopy the print (if it is a black-and-white print, copy it on a color copier to get

What's With the Paper?

Paper is a wonderful medium to use in photo crafting, but not all paper is the same. Here is a quick review of some papers you might like to use while creating with your photos.

Acetate: thin, flexible sheet of transparent plastic

Board: paper generally used for file folders, displays and postcards

Bond: paper generally used for writing, printing and photocopying

Buffered: made in an acid environment and then buffered on the surface to obtain a required pH

Cardboard: general term for stiff, bulky paper such as index, tag or Bristol

Coated: papers with a finish or coating that can be glossy or matte

Corrugated: fluted paper between sheets of paper or cardboard, or the fluted paper by itself

Dry gum: label paper or sheet of paper with glue on one side that can be activated by water

Handmade: sheet of paper made individually by hand using a mold and deckle

Index: lightweight board paper for writing and easy erasure

Mulberry: Made from the Sa-tree, this handmade paper contains coarse fibers that create a feathery look when the paper is torn or ripped.

Origami: very lightweight paper designed to crease or fold well

Parchment: paper that imitates writing "papers" made from animal skins

Quilling: lightweight paper, usually brightly colored, cut into very thin strips that are rolled into coils and shaped

Rice: A misnomer that is applied to lightweight Oriental papers, the name may be derived from the rice sizing once used in Japanese papermaking.

Tissue: thin, translucent, lightweight paper

Vellum: stiff, translucent paper available clear, colored, printed or embossed

Velveteen: paper with velvet nap and feel

Watercolor: Hot press is used for stamping because it is smooth; cold press is bumpy and is used mostly for painting. It has a high wet strength, meaning it doesn't lose strength when water is absorbed.

Waterleaf: paper with little or no sizing, making it very absorbent

richer gray tones), then add subtle strokes to add touches of color. If you have your print copied onto a heavy card stock or watercolor paper (printable watercolor papers are available at most art or computer stores), you can also use watercolor pencils to give the effect of hand coloring. You'll softly stroke color into one area of the image and then using a small damp paintbrush or waterbrush, you'll add just a touch of water to allow the pencil color to flow or blend as watercolors do so beautifully.

Magical Mosaics

You've probably seen beautiful mosaics used to create stepping-stones, table tops, candleholders and wall art, but did you ever think of creating a mosaic with your photos? Somehow all the little pieces add up to big results! You can create your own mosaic by selecting the photos you want to include. Decide on how big you want each "tile" to be and start cutting! Large or small pieces do give different effects so you may want to look through some photo crafting books or do an Internet search for inspiration.

Give yourself plenty of working area, as you will want to keep some kind of order to the photo pieces. Once you have enough photos cut to fill in your surface you can start gluing. Use a paper glue or double-sided tape. Leave a hint of a border or space between the photo pieces as you adhere each to a heavy-weight background paper. You can use several photos or have a single photo

enlarged. If you don't feel comfortable enough to "wing it" on your own, there are photo mosaic templates available at craft, scrapbooking and Internet stores. Photos take on a different feel when cut up and then pieced together again.

Weave an Image

Weaving with strips from a photo is a unique way to add dimension and pattern to a photo-crafting design. Most of us learned the basics of weaving in grade school while creating place mats and Valentine hearts that only our moms could really appreciate! The easiest technique to learn (or re-learn) is the process of "over one, under one."

A few weaving terms to become familiar with:

Loom—the frame used for weaving the piece.

Warp—the pieces that run from top to bottom (up and down).

Weft—the pieces than run across the *warp* (side to side).

Web—the single or whole piece created by weaving.

You'll need two identical photos, a personal trimmer or craft knife with ruler and self-healing cutting mat, and adhesive. The first photo will act as the loom as well as the warp. On the back of the photo, measure and mark ¼ inch, ½ inch or 1 inch (depending on the size of the photo) from what will be the top and both sides. Do not cut beyond these marks or your loom will fall apart. The warp pieces can be cut straight or curved, with all of them the same width or different widths. Cut the weft strips from the second photo (straight or curved). To make it easier,

you can draw and number the curved pieces on the back before cutting them.

Begin weaving the first row by placing one strip of weft over one warp and under the next warp, and repeat to the end of the row. The second row starts with placing a weft strip under one warp and over the next warp and repeat to the end of the row. Keep the weft strips pushed toward the top of the loom. Alternate row one and row two until the web is complete. Secure woven ends with a touch of glue. Now you are ready to use your woven photo as is or as an element of scrapbooking, card making, paper art, collage and other fun creations.

Wild & Wacky Effects

If you enjoy working with a computer, software like Photoshop, Picture It! and other photo-editing applications include a wonderful creative tool called a filter. The filter can be applied to an image or part of an image. Filters can be fairly simple effects used to mimic traditional photographic filters (which are pieces of colored glass or gelatine placed over the lens to absorb specific wavelengths of light), or they can be complex programs used to create astounding artistic effects. Using filters is a creative way to alter photos for crafting.

You can create 3-D effects, instant sepia or aging, watercolor, colored foil, kaleidoscope or even a linen texture to your photos, all with a click of a mouse! The photos can be printed out on a variety of surfaces including watercolor paper, fabric, acetate transparencies, handmade paper, specialty papers and, of course, photo

Original snapshot

Glass filter

Canvas filter

paper. Most software allows you to temporarily apply the filter to your scanned or digital photo so you can see if you like it before saving it as a permanent file. Remember to always keep the original file untouched. You can do this by saving the filtered photo under a different file name.

Delightful Decoupage

This traditional technique can be applied to photo crafting with excellent results. You can decoupage a photo or a photocopied photo. Make sure when you are using photocopies that you always test a small area of the photocopy to make sure the ink is permanent. Decoupage is traditionally done by adhering a print (in this case a photo) to a surface, usually wood. The wooden piece should be well prepared by sanding away rough edges and making sure all dust and dirt is wiped away. You'll need a paintbrush, decoupage medium or sealer plus a wooden surface. Apply a thin film of the decoupage glue to the wooden surface and place the photo on top. Gently press the photo, making sure there are no bumps, wrinkles or air bubbles underneath. Apply a second coat of decoupage medium, covering the entire surface including the top of the photo.

Add several more coats of decoupage medium, allowing each coat to dry completely. Decoupage can also be applied to paper and glass surfaces, but decoupage medium will not permanently adhere to most plastics.

Copyrights Issues

Thinking of selling your photo

Sepia filter

crafts? If using your own photos that have been taken by you, a friend or someone in your family, you have nothing to worry about when it comes to copyright laws. Professional photographers, however, own all the rights to photographs (even though you have purchased the photographs themselves), and you may not use their photographs for commercial use. In other words, you may not sell for profit anything using their photos. You must request permission from a photographer to use a photo and you must get a release form from them to do so.

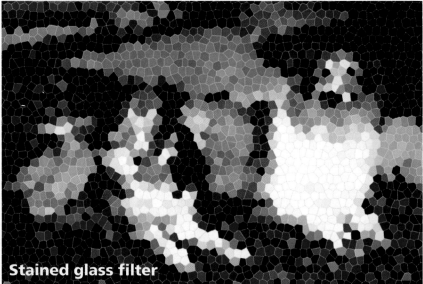

Stained glass filter

Watercolor filter

Memories of Notre Dame

Design by SUSAN STRINGFELLOW

Don't put those Paris vacation photos away in a drawer! Keep your vacation fresh in your mind by displaying a favorite photo on an altered CD!

MATERIALS

Blank CD

Black and tan card stock

Harlequin and sheet music patterned papers

Black, gold and ivory fibers

Thin gold cord

Black solvent-based ink pad

Alphabet rubber stamps

Metallic gold fabric

Gold heart charm

Gold fleur-de-lis charm

Gold dimensional letters

Small gold clamshell clip

Black and gold beads

Sanding block

Clear adhesive dots

Craft glue

Craft knife

Photo from Paris

Magnets (optional)

Lightly sand the CD; adhere harlequin patterned paper to bottom half of CD and sheet music paper to top half. Trim edges even with CD. Apply black ink to edges.

Cut three 17-inch lengths of coordinating fibers and one 17-inch length of gold cord. Wrap them around center of the CD and hold them together at side with clamshell clip. Attach several beads and the heart charm to the cord ends.

Cut a square of gold fabric and adhere to lower right corner of CD. Cut photo to 2⅛ x 2¹⁵⁄₁₆ inches; adhere to tan card stock and cut out leaving a ⅛-inch border. Adhere to black card stock; cut out leaving a ⅛-inch border.

Attach layered photo to CD with adhesive dots; adhere fleur-de-lis charm to bottom of photo. Stamp the words "Notre Dame" on an angle in upper left area of CD. Sand the tops of the "P," "A," "R," "I" and "S" dimensional letters and attach them on a diagonal in lower left area to spell "PARIS." If desired, attach magnets to back of CD. ■

SOURCES: Patterned papers by Me & My Big Ideas and Sandylion; ink pad from Tsukineko; dimensional letters from Walnut Hollow; clamshell clip from FoofaLa; adhesive dots from Glue Dots.

Wine of Italy

Design by SUSAN STRINGFELLOW

Showcase a favored vacation photo by enhancing it with coordinating embellishments.

Cut a small piece of card stock and adhere over center hole in CD. Use a palette knife to cover the entire surface of the CD with textured paint; let dry completely. Place border stencil near the center of the CD and apply a generous layer of textured paint over stencil; remove stencil carefully and allow paint to dry. Paint surface with tan acrylic paint; brush on dark tan paint for dimension. Using a craft sponge, apply brown ink to raised areas.

Adhere a strip of decorative cord below stenciled area; trim excess. Cut photo to 2 x 2¾ inches; layer onto tan card stock and trim leaving a small border. Apply brown ink to edges. Cut four 8-inch pieces of coordinating fibers and tie around photo. Adhere photo angled on left side of CD using foam tape.

Insert mini brads into centers of the silk flowers; attach flowers to right side of CD. Stamp the phrase "il vino di Italia" (the wine of Italy) along side of photo and stamp "merlot" above the stenciled border. If desired, attach magnets to the back of CD. ■

SOURCES: Textured dimensional paint and acrylic paints from Delta; ink pad from Tsukineko; rubber stamps from Hero Arts; stencil from Plaid.

MATERIALS

Blank CD
Textured dimensional paint
Tan and dark tan acrylic paints
Craft sponge
Palette knife
Tan card stock
Brown solvent-based ink pad
Small alphabet rubber stamps
2 small silk flowers
Mini brads
Cream decorative cord
Coordinating fibers
Decorative border stencil
Tacky craft glue
Adhesive foam tape
Small photo
Magnets (optional)

Beautiful Butterfly

Design by SUSAN STRINGFELLOW

Beaded fringe adds funky fun to an altered CD that doubles as a suncatcher!

MATERIALS

Blank CD

Pink card stock

Green textured paper

Coordinating striped paper

Textured silver metal scrapbook molding

Coordinating beaded trim

Dark pink fibers

Black solvent-based ink pad

Nature-quote rubber stamp

Acrylic paints: pink, green and orange

Paintbrush

Silver mini brad

Sanding block

Transparency sheet

Craft glue

Foam mounting tape

Nature photo

Magnets (optional)

Lightly sand the CD; adhere green textured paper to lower half of CD and striped paper to upper half. Trim edges even with CD. Cut a 5-inch-long strip of metal scrapbook molding; paint molding with green paint and let dry. Paint the raised areas of molding with orange and pink paints; let dry. Sand the surface lightly to expose the metal. Center and attach molding to CD; trim excess.

Adhere pink fiber around entire perimeter of CD. Cut photo to desired size; layer onto pink card stock. Trim pink card stock leaving a small border; sand edges. Attach beaded trim behind bottom edge of card stock. Stamp nature-quote image onto a transparency sheet; cut a rectangle around words and attach to bottom right corner of photo with silver brad. Adhere photo to CD with foam mounting tape. If desired, attach magnets to the back of the CD. ■

SOURCES: Striped paper from KI Memories; scrapbook moulding and mini brad from Making Memories; fibers from Fibers By The Yard; ink pad from Tsukineko; rubber stamp from Stampin' Up!.

Summer Memories

Design by JEANNE WYNHOFF

Create a summer background on a CD that commemorates a special vacation.

Cut a 5-inch square from blue patterned paper; use a glue stick to attach paper to CD. Trim edges even. Cut nautical patterned fabric 5 x 4½ inches; run through adhesive machine and attach to CD. Trim excess edges. Cut fish net 5 x 2½ inches; attach to left side of CD with adhesive dots.

Cut out a starfish and sand dollar from nautical patterned fabric; adhere both to card stock and cut out. Attach to CD with adhesive dots. Adhere fiber around edge of CD with craft glue. Cut photos to desired sizes; use adhesive dots to attach photos and sea-horse charm to CD. ∎

SOURCES: Patterned paper from Provo Craft; adhesive cartridge and applicator from Xyron; adhesive dots from Glue Dots.

Photo Holder

Design by JAN DAVENPORT

Make your own photo holder by adding funky clips and pretty paper to an extra CD. Add a magnet or attach a stand for display.

MATERIALS

Blank CD
Small photos
Green textured paper
Small antique silver metal frame
Rub-on word transfer
Clear word stickers
Gold embossing powder
Clear dimensional embossing enamel
Embossing ink pad
Silver and gold spiral clips
Green fibers
Used postage stamps
Magnets
Heat embossing tool
Drill with drill bits
Craft knife
Craft glue

Adhere textured paper to CD cutting out center hole with craft knife. Drill two holes toward the top of the CD; thread fiber through holes and tie into a bow. Attach a piece of fiber toward CD bottom; rub edges of CD with embossing ink, coat with gold embossing powder and melt powder with heat embossing tool.

Adhere a photo on the reverse side of the CD so the image shows through the center; adhere metal frame over center hole to frame photo. Embellish frame with rub-on transfers, word stickers and postage stamps. Cover frame front with embosing ink. Coat with clear dimensional embossing enamel and melt powder with heat tool. Attach small photos to sides of CD with spiral clips; attach additional spiral embellishments as desired. Glue magnets to back of CD. ∎

SOURCES: Metal frame and rub-on word transfer from Making Memories; clear word stickers from Creative Imaginations; swirl clips from 7 Gypsies.

Winter Memories

Design by RACHAEL GIALLONGO

Chunky iridescent glitter creates the everlasting snow that borders this fun CD photo holder!

Cut a 3-inch piece of ribbon; fold in half to form a loop and adhere to front of CD. Glue a piece of denim blue card stock to CD covering glued ribbon; trim edges even with CD. Paint edges white; apply embossing powder and emboss. Apply glue to edges of CD; roll edges on a paper plate filled with chunky iridescent glitter. Apply "Winter" rub-on transfer toward bottom of CD; apply embossing powder to word and emboss.

Insert light blue thread into sewing needle; thread button and complete a few stitches through holes. Tie a knot on front of button. Adhere chosen photos to CD and embellish with button, safety pin and spiral paper clip. Use label maker and label tape to make desired year sticker; add to bottom of photo. Attach photo corners where desired. ∎

SOURCES: Card stock, embossing powder and ribbon from Close To My Heart; label maker from Dymo; safety pins and rub-on transfer from Making Memories.

MATERIALS
Blank CD
Denim blue card stock
Label maker with label tape
Blue button
Small safety pin
Sewing needle
Light blue thread
"Winter" rub-on transfer
White acrylic paint
White embossing powder
Embossing heat tool
Chunky iridescent glitter
Blue gingham ribbon
Silver photo corners
Spiral paper clip
Paintbrush
Craft glue
Paper plate
Photos

Son Tag

Design by S A N D R A G R A H A M S M I T H

Tuck a black and white photo in the little pocket on the front of this tag. A border punch adds a lace-look border that adds to the vintage feel of this project.

MATERIALS

Card stock: light brown, olive green and black

1½-inch square black envelope

2 antique brass eyelets

Lace border punch

Alphabet typewriter rubber stamps

Black ink pad

Black tassels: 1 small and 1 large

3 (⅝-inch) self-adhesive clear pebbles

Dictionary printed paper with the words "family" and "child"

Small hole punch

Glue stick

Small black and white photo

Using pattern provided, cut out a large tag shape from olive green card stock. Cut two 1½ x 3-inch pieces of black card stock; punch a lace border in one piece and glue to bottom of tag. Trim edges. For remaining piece, punch the lace border at one end and trace around the top of the tag on the remaining end. Glue to top of tag; trim excess. Punch a small hole at top of tag; attach an eyelet and thread large black tassel through eyelet.

Using pattern provided, cut out a small tag shape from light brown card stock. Glue photo onto tag; punch a hole at top and attach an eyelet. Thread small black tassel through eyelet and glue to secure. Referring to photo for placement, glue the black envelope to large tag and insert the small tag inside the envelope.

Cut out "child" and "family" definitions from dictionary printed paper; glue "child" paper at an angle on tag. Layer "family" paper onto black card stock; cut a small border and layer again onto light brown card stock. Cut a small border and glue to tag.

Use black ink to stamp the word "son" onto light brown card stock; cut out each letter separately leaving a small border. Referring to photo for placement, glue letters to tag and attach a clear pebble on top of each. ∎

SOURCES: Rubber stamps from River City Rubber Works; patterned paper from K&Company.

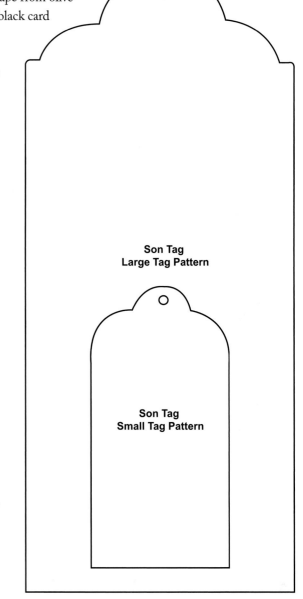

**Son Tag
Large Tag Pattern**

**Son Tag
Small Tag Pattern**

Sunshine Tag

Design by MARY AYRES

Tell a special someone that she's the center of your universe by featuring her face in the center of a blazing sun!

MATERIALS

Card stock: orange, light orange, yellow and turquoise

Clear vellum

White fibers

Craft thread: yellow, light orange and orange

3 (³⁄₁₆-inch) yellow washer eyelets

Instant-dry paper adhesive

1¼- and ³⁄₁₆-inch circle punches

4 varying decorative-edge scissors

Small photo

Computer font (optional)

Cut a 3 x 5½-inch rectangle from turquoise card stock; trim top corners diagonally to form a tag. Punch a ³⁄₁₆-inch hole centered at top of tag; attach eyelet. Cut five 8-inch pieces from each color of craft thread. Hold all the pieces together with ends even; fold in half and insert ends through eyelet from back to front. Bring ends back through formed loop and pull taut against tag.

Glue white fibers horizontally and unevenly across tag; trim ends. Punch a 1¼-inch circle from desired area of photo. Use decorative-edge scissors to cut a 1¾-inch circle from yellow card stock; cut a 2¼-inch circle from light orange card stock with another pair of decorative-edge scissors. Cut a 2¾-inch circle from orange card stock, using a different pair of decorative-edge scissors. Layer circles and adhere together so they are slightly off-center. Adhere assembled circle to tag; trim edge of largest circle even with tag.

Use a computer or hand-print "Sunshine" on vellum; cut a ⅞ x 3-inch rectangle around word, cutting top edge with remaining pair of decorative-edge scissors. Position vellum word on bottom of tag ¼ inch from edge; punch a ³⁄₁₆-inch hole in both ends of vellum and attach eyelets. ■

SOURCES: Eyelets from Creative Impressions; Zip Dry paper adhesive from Beacon.

Key Tag

Design by SHARON REINHART

Acrylic self-adhesive shapes aren't just for scrapbooking! Adhere one to a favorite photo and add a key ring for a quick project that's also useful.

Adhere clear tag to desired area of photo; trim away excess photo. Punch a hole through photo using tag hole as a guide. Open jump ring on key chain with pliers; attach photo tag and close jump ring. ■

SOURCES: Clear tag from K&Company.

MATERIALS

Key chain
Small self-adhesive clear tag
⅛-inch hole punch
Pliers
Small photo

Woven-Look Bookmark Set

Designs by Sharon Reinhart

Save your unusable photos to use in this technique that resembles intricate weaving!

MATERIALS

Clear and yellow vellum
Green and white card
   stock
Rubber stamps: "Take
   Time to Enjoy" and
   "love"
Brown ink pad
Brown fibers
Small square wooden
   bead
3 inches thin craft wire
2 black mini brads
Brown eyelet
Eyelet setter and small
   hammer
Paper trimmer
¼-, ⅛- and ¹⁄₁₆-inch hole
   punches
1¼-inch circle punch
Daisy punch
Double-sided adhesive
   sheets
Mini adhesive dots
Desired photos

TAKE TIME BOOKMARK

Cut adhesive sheet 2 x 5½ inches; adhere to a piece of green card stock cut to the same size. Use paper trimmer to cut desired photo into ⅛-inch strips horizontally. Remove remaining liner from adhesive sheet on bookmark; adhere one photo strip diagonally across center of bookmark. Adhere two to three additional strips next to first strip; adhere two to three more in opposite direction. Continue adding strips, changing direction as desired, until bookmark is entirely covered in an abstract pattern. Trim photo strips even with edges of bookmark.

Cut clear vellum 1½ x 5½ inches; stamp sentiment onto center of vellum and let dry. Position vellum on bookmark; punch a ¹⁄₁₆-inch hole at top and bottom, and insert brads.

DAISY LOVE BOOKMARK

Create the abstract patterned bookmark base by following the instructions for the previous bookmark.

Stamp "love" sentiment onto yellow vellum; punch out with circle punch. Lay stamped circle at top of bookmark; punch a ⅛-inch hole at top and attach eyelet. Fold a 6-inch length of fiber in half; insert through eyelet from back to front creating a loop. Pull fiber tails through loop; string wooden bead onto fibers and tie a knot. ***Note:*** *Use a small piece of wire folded in half to help guide the fibers through the bead.*

Punch six daisies from yellow vellum; adhere two together to make three layered daisies in total. Punch three ¼-inch holes from photo; adhere to center of daisies. Adhere daisies to bottom of bookmark. ■

SOURCES: Rubber stamp from Hero Arts.

Wishes Bookmark

Design by MARTHA BLEIDNER

Cut out an area of an otherwise less-than-perfect photo to use as the focal point of this colorful bookmark.

MATERIALS

Purple and light purple
    card stock

Iridescent vellum

2 3-D star stickers

⅛-inch-wide satin ribbon:
    purple and light purple

¼-inch hole punch

Vellum tape

Paper adhesive

Desired photo

Computer font (optional)

Cut a 1 x 2-inch rectangle from desired area of photo. Cut a 1⅝ x 8½-inch strip of light purple card stock; cut a 2⅛ x 8½-inch strip of purple card stock. Adhere light purple strip to purple strip; adhere photo to top portion of light purple strip.

Use a computer or hand print "WISHES" vertically on iridescent vellum; cut a rectangle around words allowing approximately an extra inch at top and bottom. Attach vellum rectangle to bookmark with vellum tape; add 3-D star stickers above and below word. Punch a hole in center top of bookmark; thread two pieces of ribbon through hole and tie. ∎

SOURCES: Stickers from Sandylion.

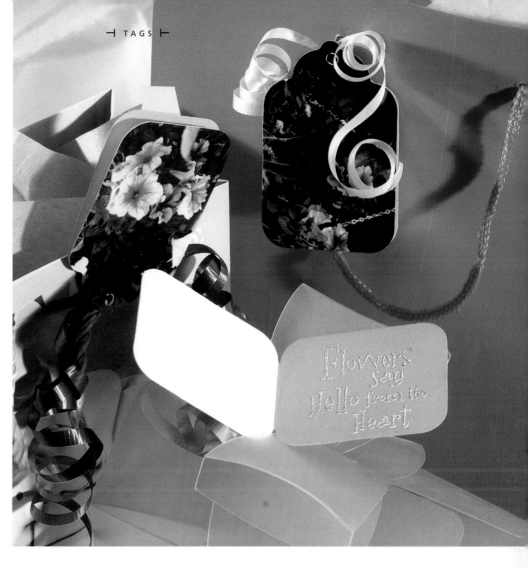

Gift Tags

Designs by SHARON REINHART

Custom-made photo tags allow you to create a tag that complements your gift. A sentiment rubber stamp adds the message inside.

Punch tag shape from photo and card stock. Stamp flower sentiment onto card-stock tag; apply embossing powder and emboss with heat tool. Using a bone folder and ruler, score a line on photo tag ½ inch from curved edge. Apply glue on the curved end of the card-stock tag and adhere tags together. Once dry, punch a ¹⁄₁₆-inch hole on the left side of tag and insert a silver brad through hole. Repeat process for desired number of tags. ■

SOURCES: Tag punch from Emagination Crafts; rubber stamp from Hero Arts.

MATERIALS

Desired photos
Coordinating-color card
    stock
Silver mini brads
Flower sentiment rubber
    stamp
Silver embossing powder
Silver pigment ink pad
Tag shape punch
¹⁄₁₆-inch hole punch
Embossing heat tool
Bone folder
Ruler
Glue stick

Vintage Photo Wall Hanging

Design by MARY LYNN MALONEY

Add a classy touch to your home with a framed vintage photo. Pretty fibers add texture.

MATERIALS

- 5½-inch square papier-mâché box lid
- Ink pads: dark brown, tan, dark pink and dark purple
- Copper leafing pen
- Sheet music
- 8 x 10-inch watercolor paper
- Ink-jet water slide decal paper
- Water spray bottle
- Small dish of warm water
- Small rubber brayer
- 3 tubular wooden beads
- 5½ inches beige beaded fringe
- Multicolored metallic yarn
- Foam brush
- Acrylic adhesive medium
- Permanent adhesive
- Fabric adhesive
- Computer with scanner and ink-jet printer

Apply tan and dark brown inks directly onto box lid in a random fashion; let dry. Color inside edges of lid with copper leafing pen; let dry.

Cut a 5½-inch square from sheet music and crumple up. Carefully smooth out paper and rub surface lightly with tan ink pad. Immediately spritz paper with water; let ink run and create darker areas of color. Let dry completely.

Scan photo on computer and print onto the ink-jet water slide decal paper following manufacturer's instructions. Let dry thoroughly for several hours.

Tear photo from decal paper and lay it in a dish of warm water. ***Note:*** *Photo will curl.* While photo is soaking in dish, tear watercolor paper to a size slightly smaller than box lid; brush a thin coat of acrylic adhesive medium onto paper. Remove photo from water and slowly slide the filmlike portion of paper onto the watercolor paper. Carefully roll over image with a rubber brayer to remove excess water and air bubbles; brush another thin layer of acrylic adhesive medium over image and let dry.

Apply dark pink and dark purple inks to torn edges of watercolor paper. Adhere sheet music paper into box lid with the acrylic adhesive medium; adhere watercolor page on top of sheet music.

Use permanent adhesive to attach three wooden beads to the top outside edge of box lid; thread metallic yarn through beads and tie into a knot a few inches above the lid, creating a hanger. Trim excess yarn. Use fabric adhesive to attach beige beaded fringe to the bottom outside edge of lid; glue a 5½-inch piece of metallic yarn on top of beaded fringe. ■

SOURCES: Copper leafing pen from Krylon; water slide decal paper from Lazertran; acrylic Perfect Paper Adhesive from USArtQuest.

Vintage Photo Set

Designs by JILL MEYER

Combine vintage photos with delicate beaded fringe for pretty Victorian-style wall art.

MATERIALS

Transfer ink
Vintage photo
Jumbo playing card
White, off-white and
    burgundy card stock
Gold embossed paper
Coordinating decorative
    paper
Gold and copper leafing
    pens
Beaded fringe trim
Flower and pearl
    embellishment
Brown picot ribbon
Lace
Walnut ink
Burgundy antiquing glaze
Printer paper
Computer and scanner
Soft rubber brayer
Corner punch
Decorative-edge scissors
Permanent adhesive
Removable tape

Use a computer and scanner to heighten the color slightly on a vintage color photograph; print out photo onto regular printer paper. ***Note:*** *If there is writing on photo, reverse image on computer before printing.* Use removable tape to attach printed-out photograph face down onto white card stock. Spray the back of the printout with transfer ink and proceed to transfer the image by rubbing the backside with a soft rubber brayer until transfer has occurred. Let image dry.

Image can now be embellished as desired. Apply gold or copper leafing to edges; layer onto chosen card stocks and papers. Adhere beaded fringe trim to the back of the photo. Apply antiquing mediums and/or walnut ink to jumbo playing card to age the surface; let dry. Adhere layered piece onto playing card. ∎

SOURCES: Glaze Vernis and corner punch from Plaid; transfer ink from Stewart Superior; gold and copper leafing pens from Krylon; gold foil paper from Artifacts Inc.; walnut ink from Tsukineko.

Photo Pocket Holder

Design by MARY AYRES

Tuck special photos and other memorabilia in the stitched pockets of this handy organizer!

Score a line across file 2 inches from top edges on front and back; fold over to outside of file for flaps. Cut two 11¾ x 1¾-inch rectangles from denim-striped patterned paper; tear one long edge on each rectangle. Glue rectangles to flaps with bottom and side edges even and torn edge at top. Using a zigzag stitch, machine-sew around sides, bottom edge and ¼ inch down from torn top edge on each flap.

Cut a 6½ x 11¾-inch rectangle from mottled tan paper. Cut three 2¼ x 3-inch rectangles from denim-striped patterned paper to act as pockets, tearing side and bottom edges. *Note: Stripes should run vertically.* Tear three 1½-inch squares from mulberry paper; adhere one square diagonally to center of each pocket. Center and attach a button sticker to each mulberry square.

Using a straight stitch, machine sew around each of the mulberry squares. Thread sewing needle and make a stitch through each of the button holes, securing ends in back with glue. Adhere pockets symmetrically across bottom of mottled tan rectangle. *Note: Place glue around bottom and side edges only, so pockets can hold photos.* Using a zigzag stitch, machine sew around sides and bottom of pockets ¼ inch from edges. Punch holes in the top corners of each pocket; attach eyelets. Insert fibers through eyelets and glue ends in back. Adhere mottled tan rectangle to front of pouch, keeping edges even.

Punch two holes through both layers on front flap 2 inches in from sides and ¾ inch down from top. Attach eyelets to holes; insert a 17-inch piece of fiber through eyelets and knot ends on inside of pouch to create a handle. Repeat process for back flap. Insert photos into pockets. ∎

SOURCES: Stickers from EK Success; Zip Dry paper adhesive from Beacon.

MATERIALS

- 8½ x 11¾-inch brown accordion-fold file
- Mottled tan paper
- Denim-striped patterned paper
- Blue mulberry paper
- Bone folder
- Blue fibers
- Button stickers
- Instant-dry paper adhesive
- 10 (⅛-inch) round antique copper eyelets
- ⅛-inch circle punch
- Rotary tool and scoring blade
- White sewing thread
- Sewing machine
- Sewing needle
- Desired photos

Photo Kaleidoscopes

Designs by DEANNA HUTCHISON

Capture the magic of the kaleidoscopes from your childhood by piecing together duplicate copies of your favorite photo.

MATERIALS

- 4 regular reprints and 4 reverse reprints of chosen photo
- 12 x 12-inch decorative scrapbook paper
- 12 x 12-inch card stock
- Coordinating scrapbook embellishments
- Ribbon
- 45-degree see-through triangle
- Ballpoint pen
- Craft knife
- Ruler
- Mounting squares

Determine section of photo that will be the focal point of design; check measurements of focal point in reprints. If there are differences, trim photos so focal points will line up evenly.

Lay a 45-degree see-through triangle over the desired section of photo on one of the regular reprints. Turn photo over and lay triangle on the backside. Use a ballpoint pen to lightly draw a line into the corner. ***Note:*** *It is very important that it lines up right into the corner to ensure exact points in the center of the kaleidoscope.* Remove triangle and hold photo up to light to ensure that line is in the correct spot before cutting.

Use craft knife and a ruler to cut on the line. Continue cutting regular reprints in same manner. To cut reversed reprints, change triangle to the opposite side.

Begin to assemble pieces by taking one regular reprint and one reversed reprint; place cut sides together and attach with mounting squares. Repeat with remaining photos. Once all pairs are attached, start to join them all together with mounting tape. ***Note:*** *If pairs do not fit together exactly at first, check measurements and trim as needed to fit.* Trim outside edges as desired.

Mount photo kaleidoscope onto card stock; trim to desired size. Mount matted kaleidoscope onto scrapbook paper. Add ribbon and coordinating scrapbook embellishments. Frame and hang as desired. ■

Inspire Frame

Design by MARY AYRES

Frame a black and white photo with corrugated paper, then add fiber and an antique button for instant vintage style.

MATERIALS

- 5½ x 7¼-inch black cardboard frame
- Brown wavy corrugated cardboard
- Brown fibers
- Orange glass pebble
- Hemp cord
- Brown feather
- Clear vellum
- Paper with printed words
- "Inspire" rub-on transfer
- Metallic gold spray paint
- Brown dye ink pad
- Craft sponge
- Paintbrush
- Fabric adhesive
- Bead adhesive
- Fine sandpaper
- 3½ x 5-inch photo

Cut a 5¼ x 7-inch rectangle from wavy corrugated cardboard and cut a 3¼ x 5-inch opening from the center. Use a craft sponge to apply brown ink to edges. Following manufacturer's instructions, spray metallic gold paint onto rectangle; when dry, glue to front of frame.

Glue a strand of fiber along left side of corrugated rectangle; glue another strand of fiber across top of rectangle. Trim ends.

Place glass pebble on paper with printed words and cut around edge. Brush a thick layer of bead adhesive onto back of pebble; adhere to paper and let dry. When dry, gently rub sandpaper across edge of paper to smooth it even with pebble. Wrap hemp cord around pebble like it is a package; knot ends together on top. Trim ends and glue pebble to top left corner of frame.

Apply a sentiment to vellum; tear a rectangle around word and glue rectangle underneath right side of pebble. Glue feather above word. ∎

SOURCES: Cardboard frame and fibers from EK Success; glass pebble from JudiKins; rub-on transfer from Royal & Langnickel; spray paint from Krylon; adhesives from Beacon.

Spring Tulips Photo Mosaic

Design by DEANNA HUTCHISON

Photos cut into little bits and pieces form a dramatic frame to a coordinating center photo. Frame this piece and display it where it will receive oohs and aahs!

MATERIALS

- 12 x 12-inch light green and dark green card stock
- Photo-safe pen
- Ruler
- Craft knife
- Adhesive mounting tabs
- Desired tulip photos

Choose one photo to be a central photo; set aside. ***Note:*** *This photo will not be cut into squares.* With a photo-safe pen and a ruler, create a grid of 1-inch squares on the back of each remaining photo. Before cutting each photo, number the squares to make it easier to reassemble them later. Cut photos into squares with a ruler and craft knife; rebuild each photo laying out squares in correct positions.

Determine center of light green card stock and adhere uncut photo in that spot. Lightly draw a straight line approximately ⅛ inch from bottom and ⅛ inch from left edge to create a border. Starting in the bottom left corner, begin to lay the first row of squares along the straight line, leaving equal space between each. Before mounting photo squares, loosely lay them all out on card stock to ensure proper spacing and alignment. Once desired layout is achieved, begin to mount bottom row by attaching an adhesive mounting tab to each square.

Once bottom row is attached, begin to mount left row, leaving same amount of space between each square as in bottom row. Once these two rows are attached, begin working out from the corner until all squares have been adhered. If necessary, trim card-stock edges; adhere to dark green card stock. ■

Bundle-of-Joy Shadowbox

Design courtesy of DUNCAN ENTERPRISES

MATERIALS

Papier-mâché shadowbox
    frame
White card stock
Light blue striped paper
Baby boy-themed
    patterned paper
Baby boy-themed stickers
Bunny die-cut
Clear rhinestone star
    stickers
Baby-themed rub-on
    transfers
Mini clothespin
Small piece of baby
    blanket
Small flower die-cuts
Wooden letter game
    pieces
Sheer blue ribbon
White satin ribbon
Adhesive foam tape
Glue stick
Craft glue
Small baby photo

Celebrate the birth of a beloved newborn by creating a shadowbox collage. Tie the project together with your favorite embellishments.

Cover the frame with blue striped paper; embellish the outside with star stickers, ribbon and desired baby-themed stickers, and rub-on transfers. Cut and adhere a piece of baby boy-themed patterned paper inside the shadowbox. Embellish paper with sheer ribbon, star stickers and rub-on transfers. Attach a small piece of baby blanket inside frame.

Choose a baby sentiment rub-on transfer and apply it to white card stock; tear edges and mount inside frame with adhesive foam tape. Add the bunny die-cut below blanket; attach baby photo to blanket with mini clothespin. Mount desired wooden letters to small pieces of white card stock; trim around edges and mount inside frame. Add small flower die-cuts around letters. ■

SOURCES: PSX patterned papers, stickers, die-cut, rhinestone star stickers and rub-on transfers from Duncan.

Homegrown Happiness

Design by S T A C E Y   W A K E L I N

Don't hide away your handcrafted cards! Add interesting embellishments and display your projects where you can see them every day.

Cut brown card stock 6 x 12 inches; score and fold in half. Use a craft knife to cut a large "x" in the center of the card; carefully tear out square to create an opening. Moisten torn edges with water and roll them slightly. Use a craft sponge to apply brown ink to edges of card.

Wrap brown fiber around right side of card, wrapping ends inside and securing with a brad at top and bottom. Attach desired stickers to brown card stock; trim edges leaving a small border. Use adhesive foam dots to attach layered stickers to card.

Apply metallic gold ink to photo corners; determine placement of corners and adhere inside card. Lightly sand photo and insert into photo corners. ■

SOURCES: Stickers from Pebbles Inc.; brads from Making Memories.

MATERIALS

Brown card stock
Coordinating word stickers
Brown fiber
2 brown mini brads
4 black photo corners
Metallic gold and brown
    ink pads
Craft sponge
Adhesive foam dots
Glue stick
Sandpaper
Craft knife
Desired photo

Memorable Tote

Design by ANNIE LANG

Carry your memories wherever you go! Add a custom-made scrapbook page to the front of any size tote bag for a bag that will generate custom-made compliments!

MATERIALS

- 15 x 16-inch canvas tote bag
- 12 x 12-inch clear sheet protector
- 12 x 12-inch patterned paper
- 12 x 12-inch mat board
- 12 x 12-inch prefinished scrapbook photo layout
- 1½ yards coordinating decorative trim
- ½-inch-wide double-sided tape
- Double-sided adhesive sheets
- Scissors

Adhere patterned paper to mat board; insert covered mat board into clear sheet protector. ***Note:*** *Punched hole tab flap on sheet protector should be trimmed off.* Use double-sided tape to hold the non-patterned side of the mat board to the sheet protector to keep it secure.

Place the sheet protector with mat board side up onto the work surface; attach adhesive sheets to the back of the protector, covering the entire surface. Trim adhesive edges as necessary.

Carefully adhere the sheet protector onto the front of the bag, pressing firmly. Measure and cut decorative trim to fit along each side of the protector; clip corners to fit together. Apply ½-inch-wide double-sided tape to the back of each trim piece; attach into place. ***Note:*** *Trim needs to cover the plastic edging and overlap onto the canvas fabric.* When attaching the top piece of trim, apply it to the back edge of the protector so pocket stays open. Insert prefinished scrapbook layout into tote bag. ∎

SOURCES: Double-sided tape and double-sided adhesive sheets from Therm O Web.

Gardening Muslin Bag

Design by KATHLEEN PANEITZ

Transfer a garden photo to a muslin bag and fill with garden-fresh potpourri to create a distinctive gift for a friend!

MATERIALS

Small muslin bag

Matte-finish soft gel gluing medium

Paintbrush

Alphabet rub-on transfers

Craft stick

Garden photo

Computer with scanner

Ink-jet paper

Ink-jet printer

Use computer and ink-jet printer to make a copy of photo. Apply a thin layer of soft gel gluing medium to the area of the muslin bag where image will be transferred. Lay photocopy, image side down, onto gel medium. Burnish back of the copy with the craft stick to transfer image to bag. Carefully begin peeling back the photocopy. **Note:** *If image has not transferred successfully in certain areas, lower copy back down and burnish area again.* Transfer a garden message to bag using rub-on alphabet. ∎

SOURCES: Muslin bag from Paper Mart; Soft Gel Matte Medium from Golden Artist Colors Inc.; rub-on transfers from Making Memories.

Birthday Gift Box

Design by HEATHER D. WHITE

Colorful punched circles add fun contrast to the square slide mount on the front of this happy greeting.

Measure and cut patterned papers to fit the front and top of the box; measure and cut solid pink paper to fit the sides of box. Lay front piece aside and attach remaining pieces to box with double-sided tape.

Begin to lay out cut and torn pieces of paper in a pleasing arrangement on front piece. Use a computer or hand-print desired birthday greeting on vellum; tear side edges of vellum and use double-sided tape to attach to paper.

Adhere circle tags onto paper; frame desired photo in metal frame and attach to design with double-sided tape. Adhere design to front of gift box; if needed, finish assembling box. ∎

SOURCES: Patterned paper and circle tags from KI Memories; frame from Making Memories; vellum from Provo Craft.

MATERIALS

White gift box
3 coordinating patterned
  papers
Solid pink paper
Clear vellum
Pre-punched coordinating
  circle tags
Small metal frame
Double-sided tape
Computer font (optional)

Heritage Bottle

Design by KAREN BLONIGEN, *courtesy of Krylon*

MATERIALS

- Gray primer spray paint
- Copper metallic spray paint
- Satin-finish varnish spray
- Spray adhesive
- Glass bottle
- Cork topper
- Vintage vellum photo die-cuts
- 4 vintage mini metal frames
- Dimensional clear typewriter alphabet and number stickers
- Silver photo corners
- 2 scrap pieces of lace
- 3 small pieces of assorted jewelry chain
- 2 vintage beads
- 10 inches sheer ribbon
- 7 small jump rings
- 2 silver eye pins
- 100-grit sandpaper
- Painter's tape
- Newspaper
- Waxed paper
- Soft cloth
- Craft glue
- Tweezers
- Long-nosed pliers
- Wire cutters

Choose your favorite vintage family photos, a few charms of your choice, and get ready to put together a wonderful family heritage piece!

Project note: To personalize the bottle, substitute family photos photocopied onto vellum in place of the vellum die-cuts.

Mask off the top of the bottle and 1 inch of the bottle neck with painter's tape. Roughen remaining surface, including the bottom, with sandpaper; wipe clean with a soft cloth.

Lay newspaper on work surface; sit bottle on top of a sheet of waxed paper. *Note: The waxed paper will allow the bottle to be turned to spray the entire surface evenly.* Following manufacturer's instructions and letting each coat dry thoroughly, spray two coats of gray primer over the entire surface of the bottle including the bottom. Spray two coats of copper metallic paint over entire surface of bottle; spray two coats of varnish onto bottle. Once completely dry, carefully remove painter's tape.

Cut a piece of lace to fit around the neck of the bottle; apply a thin line of craft glue around the neck partially on the unfinished glass. Adhere lace. Repeat process for bottom edge of bottle; let dry.

Cut two small images from the vellum die-cuts to fit into two mini metal frames. Using tweezers to hold the images, spray the backsides with adhesive and press into frames. Attach dimensional typewriter stickers to remaining frames; set aside.

Choose a vellum die-cut to be the main image and attach desired dimensional number stickers toward bottom of image. Adhere photo corners; trim image if needed. Adhere die-cut to front of bottle; let dry.

Center and insert one eye pin into the top of the cork. Use long-nosed pliers to attach jump rings to one end of each piece of jewelry chain; secure chains to the eye pin at top of bottle. Use wire cutters to cut chains to desired lengths. Attach a jump ring to each mini frame. Thread one jewelry chain with a bead and attach a mini frame at the end of the chain. Attach one of the alphabet frames to a chain; thread remaining bead onto remaining eye pin and attach to last chain. Thread ribbon through top eye pin; tie remaining mini frames to each end of ribbon. Trim ribbon as needed. ∎

SOURCES: Primer spray, spray paint, spray adhesive and spray varnish from Krylon; vellum die-cuts and mini metal frames from MPR Associates; dimensional stickers from K&Company.

Tribal Memories Checkbook Cover

MATERIALS

- Clear plastic checkbook cover with white cardstock insert
- Textured beige paper
- Zebra-print paper
- Metallic gold tissue paper
- Clear iridescent paper
- 12 inches raffia
- Glue stick
- Craft glue
- Aluminum foil
- Small photo

Design by JUDITH ATWELL

Keep members of your tribe close at hand on the cover of a checkbook enhanced with animal-print papers!

Remove checkbook insert from plastic sleeve; lay insert right side up on a piece of aluminum foil. Tear assorted papers into small pieces and arrange on cover into a collage design with overlapping pieces. Once insert is covered, begin to adhere pieces with a glue stick.

Cut a small piece of clear iridescent paper slightly larger than desired photo; glue to back of photo. Glue layered photo to the front of the insert. With craft glue, run two lines of glue across collage; place strands of raffia onto lines of glue and press with fingers until secure.

Once collage is dry, trim all edges. Fold collage in half and insert into plastic sleeve. ∎

SOURCES: Clear checkbook cover from Neato Stuff.

Keepsake Photo Jewelry

Pendant and pin by J U D I K A U F F M A N *and bracelet by*
T R A C I A W I L L I A M S, *all designs courtesy of Sulyn*

Keep your loved ones close at hand and heart with this jewelry set created with tiny frames and your most treasured photos!

Use pattern template on jewelry packaging to trace and cut out photos in the sizes needed. Dab a small amount of clear sealer onto the flat area of one jewelry link; press photo into place. Once all photos have been adhered, lay jewelry on a flat surface. Coat each photo surface with the clear sealer. Check for any air bubbles that might result. If any are found, prick with a pin; let sealer dry overnight. Attach charms to the charm pin; add a jump ring to the pendant so it can be attached on a chain, ribbon or cording. ∎

SOURCES: Keepsake jewelry and clear sealer from Sulyn.

MATERIALS
- Keepsake bracelet
- Silver pendant
- Small silver frame charms
- Charm pin
- Clear sealer
- Small photos
- Sewing pin
- Jump ring
- Needle-nose pliers

Metallic Christmas Ornament

Design by JUDITH ATWELL

Pull out last year's Christmas cards to recycle into shimmering ornaments that feature photos of your friends and family. What better way to decorate a tree?

MATERIALS

Recycled Christmas card featuring a flower
Gold metallic tagboard
8–12 inches gold metallic craft wire
2 gold eyelets
6 red glass beads
5 red rhinestones
3½ inches gold metallic fringe
Gold glitter pen
Hole punch
Glue stick
Craft glue
Desired photo to fit into flower image

Cut flower section from Christmas card; cut tagboard to same size. Glue gold fringe to the inside bottom of the tagboard; glue Christmas card on top, lining up edges. Punch two small holes at top and set a gold eyelet into each.

Cut desired photo into a circle to fit inside flower image; glue photo to card. Trace around photo with gold glitter pen; place dots of glitter randomly on card and center a red rhinestone in each dot. Let dry.

Bend gold wire into a hanger shape; insert one end into each eyelet and twist wire into loops to secure. Add beads and twists, ending both ends of wire in a loop to secure beads. ∎

Christmas Ornaments

Design by SHARON REINHART

Decorate your holiday tree with all your favorite people. These ornaments are a great way to use small school photos!

For each ornament, cut out two ornament shapes from card stock using template and craft knife. Use gold ink to stamp Christmas script writing onto one side of each ornament shape; apply embossing powder and emboss with heat tool. Stamp bow image onto matching-color card stock and emboss; cut out, leaving a small border.

Cut an 8-inch piece of gold thread; fold in half and tie a knot at opposite end from fold. With wrong sides together, adhere ornament shapes sandwiching gold thread knot at top. Use an adhesive foam square to attach the embossed bow. Adhere tinsel shreds to center of ornament front. Punch photo out with circle punch; adhere photo on top of tinsel with a foam square. ■

SOURCES: Ornament template from Fiskars; rubber stamps from Delta/Rubber Stampede and PSX/Duncan; iridescent tinsel shreds from DeNami Design.

MATERIALS

Red and green card stock
Christmas ornament template
Christmas script writing and bow rubber stamps
Gold pigment ink pad
Gold embossing powder
Embossing heat tool
Iridescent tinsel shreds
Metallic gold thread
1¼-inch circle punch
Adhesive foam squares
Glue stick
Ruler
Craft knife
Small photos

Mosaic Greeting Card

Design by SHARON REINHART

Cut a photo into little squares to resemble painted tiles. A bit of vellum on top of one of the squares adds space for a message while letting the beauty of the photo shine through!

MATERIALS

Ivory and dark green
    card stock
Ivory embossed
    plaid paper
Clear vellum
4 gold mini brads
Sentiment rubber stamp
Brown ink pad
1/16-inch circle punch
Adhesive foam tape
Glue stick
Photo-safe pen
Ruler
Desired photo

Cut ivory card stock 4¼ x 8½ inches; score and fold in half. Cut a 3⅞-inch square of ivory embossed plaid paper; adhere to a 4-inch square of dark green card stock. ***Note:*** *Cut embossed paper to include nine squares.*

Cut desired area of photo into a 3-inch square; use photo-safe pen and ruler to create a 1-inch square grid on back of photo. Number each square and cut apart. Adhere a photo square to each one of the squares in the embossed square; adhere in numerical order to reassemble photo.

Cut a 1-inch square from vellum; stamp sentiment image to center of vellum. Let dry; adhere with glue stick over center square.

Punch a 1/16-inch hole in each corner of assembled square; insert gold brads and adhere to card using foam tape. ■

SOURCES: Embossed paper from Lasting Impressions for Paper Inc.; rubber stamp from Hero Arts.

Bloom

Design by MARY AYRES

Choose background papers to match a photo of your favorite blossoms. A buttoned-on tag sets the tone with a custom-printed sentiment.

Cut a 10 x 7-inch rectangle from light gray card stock; score and fold in half. Cut a 5 x 3-inch rectangle from light purple card stock and tear the long edges. Emboss vertical wave lines on rectangle; use a craft sponge to apply purple ink to rectangle. Glue rectangle vertically to card.

Cut flower photo into a 3¼ x 4¾ rectangle; cut same-size rectangles from dark gray and black card stock. Glue dark gray rectangle to back of photo slightly to the left and above; glue black rectangle to back of photo slightly to the right and below.

Cut a 4 x 5½-inch piece of white card stock; glue layered photo to center of white card stock. Glue to card on top of purple rectangle.

Cut a 1¼ x 3-inch rectangle from medium purple card stock and trim corners to create a tag shape. Emboss fabric texture on tag; apply purple ink to tag. Transfer the rub-on flower sentiment to a piece of vellum; tear tag shape around word and glue onto card-stock tag. ***Note:*** *Place glue under area that will be covered by the button.* Glue button to left side of vellum; glue tag to card. ∎

SOURCES: Rub-on transfer from Royal & Langnickel; texture embossing plates and embossing tool from Fiskars; Zip Dry paper adhesive from Beacon.

MATERIALS

Card stock: white, black, light gray, dark gray, light purple and medium purple
Clear vellum
⁷⁄₁₆-inch flat pink button
Flower sentiment rub-on transfer
Texture embossing plates: waves and fabric
Large-tip embossing tool
Purple dye ink pad
Craft sponge
Instant-dry paper adhesive
Rotary tool and scoring blade
Flower photo

Variations on a Calla Lily

Designs by JACQUELINE JONES

Snap some shots of your most colorful and beautiful flowers to create cards for any occasion!

MATERIALS

Wallet-size calla lily photo
Photo paper
4¼ x 5½-inch cards
Green textured, white
    textured, light purple,
    purple, green, dark
    green and white
    card stock
Green and purple buttons
Coordinating square and
    round brads
"happy birthday" rubber
    stamp
Purple chalk ink pad
Glue stick
Adhesive dots
Double-sided tape
Computer and scanner

Calla Lily Birthday

Use a computer and scanner to print wallet-size photo onto photo paper; trim leaving a small border. Adhere to purple card stock; trim edges leaving a ⅛-inch border. Cut a 4¼ x 5¼-inch piece of green card stock; tear one long edge and adhere on card front lining up top edges. Adhere matted photo to left side of card. Stamp "happy birthday" in bottom right corner; attach two buttons with adhesive dots.

Small Color-Blocks Calla Lily

Use a computer and scanner to print wallet-size photo onto photo paper; trim leaving a small white border. Cut a 1¾ x 2¾-inch strip of green card stock; cut another strip the same size of dark green card stock. Line strips up behind photo and adhere.

Cut a 3¾ x 4-inch piece of purple card stock; tear short edge and adhere to left side of card. Cut a 1½ x 4-inch piece of green card stock; tear short edge and adhere to right side of card. Referring to photo, mount image and attach two green buttons with adhesive dots.

Large Color-Blocks Calla Lily

Score and fold an 8½ x 11-inch sheet of white card stock in half to form a 5½ x 8½-inch card. Choose four colors of card stock and cut a 2⅝ x 4-inch rectangle from each color. Use double-sided tape to attach them to card in a color-block pattern.

Use a computer and scanner to enlarge calla lily photo to approximately 4 x 6 inches; print onto white textured card stock. Trim edges leaving no border. Adhere photo to white card stock and tear edges. Mount onto card front; attach assorted brads beside image. ∎

SOURCES: Rubber stamp from Stampola; chalk ink pad from Clearsnap.

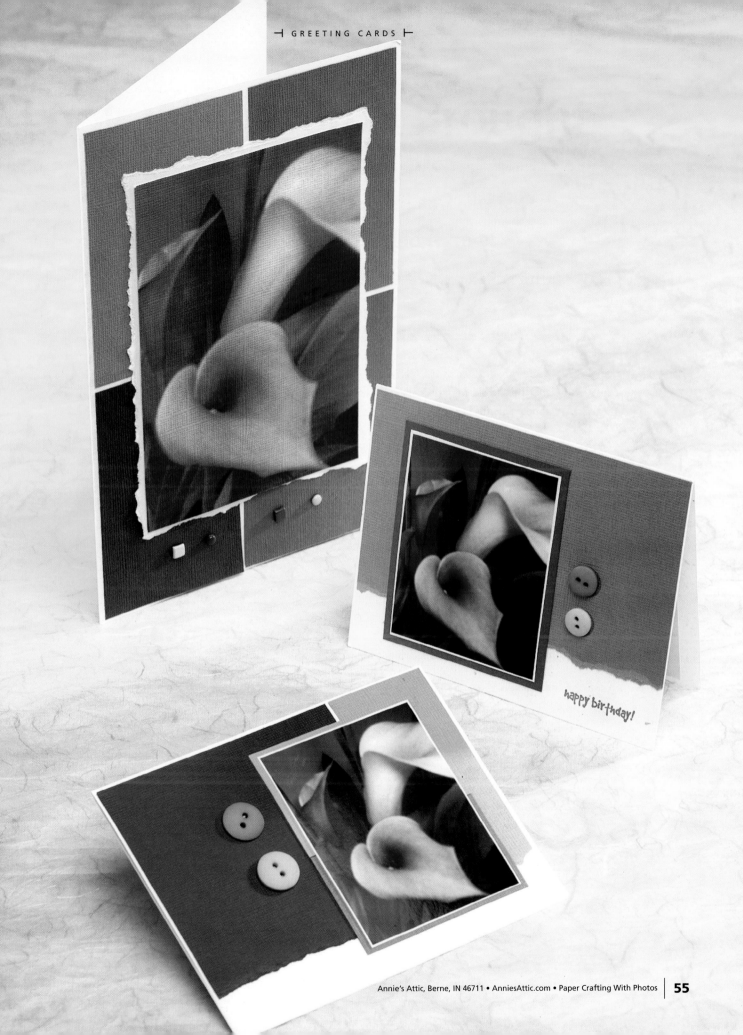

happy birthday!

Hydrangea Cards

Designs by JACQUELINE JONES

Pretty floral snapshots suit a variety of special occasions when used as the focal point of greeting cards.

MATERIALS

Card stock: white, dark green, light blue, dark blue, dark purple and light purple
White vellum
3 x 5-inch hydrangea photo
Decorative corner punch
Butterfly rubber stamp
Fine iridescent glitter
Glue stick
Glue pen
Adhesive dots
Computer and scanner
Adhesive cartridge and applicator

3-D Butterfly & Hydrangea

Use a computer and scanner to print hydrangea photo onto vellum; trim leaving a ⅛-inch border. Print "Happy Birthday" in several fonts with purple ink onto white card stock. Apply adhesive to hydrangea image and adhere on top of printed white card stock. Trim card stock to fit photo; punch corners with decorative corner punch.

Cut a 5 x 6½-inch piece of white card stock; score and fold in half. Referring to photo, cut and mount a piece of dark blue card stock to card. Layer a light blue rectangle on top followed by a dark purple rectangle. Finish by mounting hydrangea image onto dark purple card stock.

Stamp butterfly image onto vellum; cut out. Apply glue to butterfly with glue pen; add iridescent glitter and shake off excess. Let dry. Attach butterfly to card with an adhesive dot; bend wings slightly to give dimension.

"Thinking of You!" Hydrangea

Use a computer to insert the words "Thinking of you!" around the top of flower image in a rounded shape. Print photo onto vellum; trim leaving a ⅛-inch border. Apply adhesive to image and adhere to purple card stock. Trim card stock leaving a ⅛-inch border; adhere to white card stock. Tear edges of white card stock and adhere layered piece to dark blue card stock. Cut a 5 x 6½-inch piece of white card stock; score and fold in half. Adhere assembled piece to card front.

"Happy Birthday" Hydrangea

Use a computer to insert the words "Happy Birthday" above image; print photo onto vellum and trim leaving a ¹⁄₁₆-inch border. Apply adhesive to image and adhere to white card stock. Trim leaving a small border. Adhere to purple card stock and trim edges. Cut two ¾ x 4½-inch strips of dark purple card stock. Referring to photo, adhere strips to the reverse side of the light purple card stock. Adhere assembled piece to dark green card stock. Cut a 5 x 6½-inch piece of white card stock; score and fold in half. Adhere layered image to card front. ∎

SOURCES: Butterfly rubber stamp from Biblical Impressions; adhesive cartridge and applicator from Xyron.

Maple Leaf

Design by MARY AYRES

While this card showcases a maple leaf, use your favorite to frame an autumn photo.

MATERIALS

Card stock: white, brown and light brown
2 (⅛-inch) round antique brass eyelets
Brown dye ink pad
Craft sponge
Off-white burlap strand
Instant-dry paper adhesive
⅛-inch circle punch
Rotary tool and scoring blade
Sewing machine with black all-purpose thread
3½ x 5-inch horizontal photo
Computer font (optional)

Cut a 5½ x 8½-inch rectangle from light brown card stock; score and fold in half. Cut a 4 x 5¼-inch rectangle from brown card stock. Using pattern provided, cut out maple leaf from brown rectangle. Apply brown ink to inside and outside edges with a craft sponge. Adhere photo on back of rectangle with image centered inside leaf; glue rectangle to card.

Machine-stitch around edge of brown rectangle and around maple leaf following dashed lines on pattern. Use a computer or hand-print "maple leaf" on white card stock; cut a ½ x 1¾-inch rectangle around words, leaving extra space on right side. Punch a ⅛-inch hole in right side of rectangle and on right side of stem; attach eyelets. Insert burlap strand through eyelets; knot ends together and trim ends. Glue word rectangle to card. ∎

SOURCE: Zip Dry paper adhesive from Beacon.

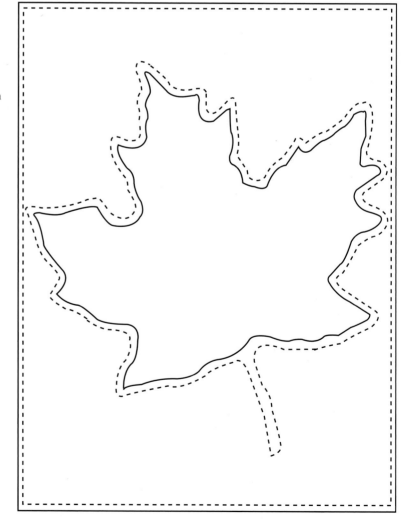

Maple Leaf Card Pattern

Two Peas in a Pod

Design by MARY AYRES

Use a circle punch to create little "peas" made from photos! Want more photos in the pod? Simply lengthen the sides to fit the number of photos you want.

MATERIALS

Card stock: white, tan, brown, bright green and dark green

Green fibers

3 (⅛-inch) round antique brass eyelets

Waves texture embossing plate

Large-tip embossing tool

1¼-inch circle punch

Brown and dark green dye ink pads

Craft sponge

Instant-dry paper adhesive

⅛-inch circle punch

Rotary tool and scoring blade

Small photos

Computer font (optional)

Cut a 5½ x 8½-inch rectangle from white card stock; score and fold in half to form card. Tear a 3½ x 4¾-inch rectangle from brown card stock; emboss wave lines onto rectangle. Use a craft sponge to apply brown ink to surface and glue to card.

Using pattern provided, trace and cut pea-pod shape from dark green card stock; glue at an angle on card. Punch two 1¼-inch faces from photos and adhere inside pod with edges of photos touching. Trace and cut the two narrow sides of the pea pod from bright green card stock; apply dark green ink to edges. Glue shapes to pea pod on card, covering sides of photos.

Glue two 1½-inch lengths of green fibers to top sides of pea pod. Use a computer or hand-print "2 peas in a pod" on tan card stock; cut a ½ x 2¼-inch rectangle around words, leaving extra space on left side. Punch a ⅛-inch hole in left side and attach an eyelet.

Punch a ⅛-inch hole on both sides of pea pod at top; attach eyelets. Insert a narrow fiber through eyelet in word rectangle and through eyelets at top of pea pod. Tie fiber into a knot and trim ends. Glue rectangle at an angle. ■

SOURCES: Texture embossing plate and embossing tool from Fiskars; Zip Dry paper adhesive from Beacon.

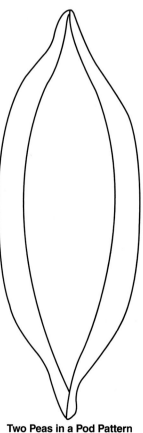

Two Peas in a Pod Pattern

2 peas in a pod

Garden Dream

Design by MARTHA BLEIDNER

A photo cut into strips of varying widths imparts a dreamy feel to the front of this card. This technique is especially effective with landscape photos!

MATERIALS

Green parchment paper
Green vellum
Iridescent vellum
Tracing paper
Vellum tape
Photo adhesive
Color copy of desired photo
Computer font (optional)

Cut green parchment paper 6½ x 11 inches; score and fold in half. Use a computer or hand-print "DREAM" on iridescent vellum; cut a rectangle around word.

Lay tracing paper over photocopy and mark desired cutting lines on paper. Cut tracing paper apart at cutting lines and use paper strips as patterns for cutting photo.

Cut three 6½-inch-long graduated strips from green vellum; adhere vertically to card with vellum tape. Position and adhere photo strips with photo adhesive; attach word rectangle with vellum tape. ■

Treasure Each Day

Design by KATHLEEN PANEITZ

Use photo pencils to draw attention to portions of a black-and-white photo. Ribbon in coordinating colors further highlights the flowers.

Cut a 5 x 8½-inch piece of pale green card stock; score and fold in half. Insert a piece of gingham ribbon through inside of card; tie into a bow on front of card and trim ends.

Following manufacturer's instructions, apply a layer of pre-color treatment photo spray to photo. Add color with photo painting pencils; adhere to white card stock. Trim white card stock leaving a small border and adhere over gingham ribbon. Apply rub-on transfer below photo. ■

SOURCES: Rub-on transfer from Making Memories; photo painting pencils and pre-color treatment photo spray from Brandess-Kalt-Aetna Group Inc.

MATERIALS

Sentiment rub-on transfer
Yellow gingham ribbon
Photo painting pencils
Pre-color treatment photo
 spray
Pale green textured card
 stock
White card stock
Paper adhesive
Wallet-size black-and-
 white photo

MATERIALS

White and dark brown textured card stock

Cork paper

Matte laminate sheet

Alphabet and life sentiment rub-on transfers

Sheer black ribbon

Spray adhesive

Color copy of a black-and-white duck photo

Spoon

Water

Shallow bowl

Enjoy Each Moment

Design by KATHLEEN PANEITZ

A black-and-white image makes a striking focal point in this card project for your favorite father!

Project Note: Even though it is a black-and-white photo, a color copy must be used to transfer image well.

Cut dark brown card stock 5½ x 8½ inches; score and fold in half. Cut a piece of laminate slightly larger than photo; peel backing from laminate sheet and lay it flat, sticky side up, on a smooth surface. Trim color copy of photo as desired. Press copy onto laminate, image side down. Burnish back of photo with the back of a spoon to make sure image is adhered to laminate.

Fill a shallow bowl with warm water; put laminate with photocopy into water and let soak for five minutes. Take image out of water and carefully begin to peel off paper copy at one corner. Peel as much of the paper off as possible being careful to not rub so hard as to rub image off laminate; let dry.

Spray adhesive on back of image and adhere to white card stock; tear card stock around photo. Adhere photo to cork paper and trim cork paper as desired. Attach to front of card.

Using alphabet rub-ons, transfer the word "Dad" to photo. Transfer the sentiment "enjoy each moment" above photo. Tie ribbon into a bow; adhere below photo. ∎

SOURCES: Rub-on transfers from Making Memories; cork paper from Magenta Rubber Stamps; laminate sheet from Xyron; spray adhesive from 3M.

Treasure & Trust

Design by MARY AYRES

Honor a true friend with a card that celebrates all the traits that make her special!

Cut a 10 x 8-inch rectangle from white card stock; score and fold in half. Apply blue ink to edges of card with a craft sponge. Transfer "Friends" sentiment onto white card stock; cut a 1 x 1¾-inch rectangle around word and apply blue ink to edges. Glue rectangle to upper left side of card.

Cut a 3¾ x 4¾-inch rectangle from white card stock; apply blue ink to edges. Adhere photo to rectangle and glue rectangle to card. Cut a rectangle from striped paper that measures 2½ x 7¾ inches. Referring to photo, trim rectangle diagonally so that height on left side of trimmed rectangle measures approximately ¾ inch. Apply blue ink to edges and adhere to bottom of card.

Trim ends of ribbon with pinking shears; glue across top of striped paper. With sewing needle and floss, thread each button; knot floss on top and trim ends. Glue one button to each ribbon end.

Transfer four sentiments onto white card stock; cut ½-inch-wide rectangles around words, leaving extra space on left side for buttons. Apply blue ink to edges. Cut rectangles from colored card stock that measure ⅛ inch larger on all sides than word rectangles; apply blue ink to edges. Glue card-stock rectangles to back of words; glue a button to each rectangle and glue rectangles diagonally underneath photo. ∎

SOURCES: Striped paper from K&Company; rub-on transfer from Royal & Langnickel; Fabri-Tac adhesive from Beacon.

MATERIALS

Card stock: white, blue, green, pink and yellow
Coordinating striped paper
Friend sentiments rub-on transfers
8½ inches (⅝-inch-wide) pink grosgrain ribbon
Pastel pink, yellow and blue buttons
White embroidery floss
Sewing needle
Blue dye ink pad
Craft sponge
Fabric adhesive
Rotary tool and scoring blade
Pinking shears
3½ x 4½-inch photo

Friends

Design by SANDRA GRAHAM SMITH

Eyelets hold the folded corners and showcase the double-sided papers that make up this fun card!

MATERIALS

Double-sided purple
    patterned paper
White card stock
White envelope
Small hole punch
8 polished aluminum
    eyelets
Silver "friends" sticker
Craft knife
Ruler
Stylus
Glue stick
Double-sided tape
Small photo

Card

Cut white card stock 4½ x 9 inches; score and fold in half. Cut a 4½-inch square from double-sided patterned paper; adhere to front of card with darker side face up. Trim edges even with card. Cut a 4-inch square from double-sided patterned paper; with lighter side face up, bend the bottom right corner up approximately ¾ inch. Punch a hole in corner; attach an eyelet. Glue square to card, lining up top and left edges.

Cut a 3½-inch square from patterned paper; with darker side face up, measure a 1-inch square in center. Score each line of the center square; cut an "x" in the center using a ruler and craft knife. Bend scored edges of square back to reveal a window opening.

Fold bottom right corner up to meet corner of opening; punch a hole in corner and attach an eyelet. Punch a hole in each opening flap; attach eyelets. Center picture in opening and attach to back of window with double-sided tape; glue square to card, lining up top and left edges. Place silver "friends" sticker on bottom right corner.

Envelope

Cut a ¾-inch-wide strip of double-sided patterned paper; with lighter side face down, fold bottom right corner up. Punch a hole and secure with an eyelet. Cut a ¾-inch square of patterned paper; adhere to bottom left corner of envelope with darker side face up. Adhere strip on top of square, lining up edges. Trim edges as needed. Repeat with another strip, only reverse dark/light colors; adhere next to first strip.

Trace envelope flap onto patterned paper; cut out and adhere to back flap. ∎

SOURCES: Sticker from Stampendous.

Welcome Baby

Design by MARY AYRES

Announce new baby's arrival with a card that features a photo! Simple stitching adds soft dimension.

MATERIALS

- White and light green card stock
- Clear vellum
- Baby sentiments rub-on transfers
- Green craft thread
- Embroidery needle
- Green dye ink pad
- Craft sponge
- Instant-dry paper adhesive
- Rotary tool and scoring blade
- 3½ x 5-inch vertical photo

Cut an 8 x 10-inch rectangle from white card stock; score and fold in half. Cut a 7½ x 4½-inch rectangle from white card stock; apply green ink to edges with a craft sponge. Glue rectangle to card. Cut a 9 x 3½-inch rectangle from light green card stock; apply green ink to edges. Tear top and bottom of photo; glue photo to upper area of light green rectangle, lining up side edges.

Using an embroidery needle, punch holes below photo ½ inch apart. Measure approximately ½ inch above holes and punch another set of holes ½ inch apart. In same manner, punch holes above photo; measure approximately ½ inch below holes and punch another set of holes ½ inch apart.

Referring to photo, thread needle and insert it in and out through holes diagonally going in both directions to form x's. Glue ends in back. Adhere assembled photo rectangle to front of card at an angle; trim edges even with card.

Transfer a baby sentiment onto vellum; cut a 1½ x 5-inch rectangle around words and tear long sides. Apply green ink to long edges. Place vellum rectangle on bottom of card. Using an embroidery needle, punch two vertical holes through vellum and card ½ inch apart on both ends. Thread needle and insert it through holes; tie into bows. Repeat for opposite end. Trim bow ends. ■

SOURCES: Rub-on transfer from Royal & Langnickel; Zip Dry paper adhesive from Beacon.

wel•come (wĕl′kəm) *adj.*
1. Received with pleasure and hospitality into one's home 2. Willing or glad acceptance

Winter Card

Design by MARY AYRES

Back a winter photo with "snow"-flecked mesh. Icy ribbon adds a wintry touch!

Cut a 10 x 7-inch rectangle from white card stock; score and fold in half. Use craft sponge to apply blue ink to edges of card. Cut a 4¾ x 6¾-inch rectangle from white card stock; apply blue ink to edges and glue to card. Cut a 5¼ x 3-inch piece of netting; trim bottom edge with pinking shears. Fold the top ½ inch of netting over top of card and glue to secure. Leave remaining netting loose.

Cut two rectangles from white card stock with one measuring 3¼ x 4¾ inches and the other measuring 3½ x 5 inches. Apply blue ink to edges; layer and adhere photo and rectangles. Wrap ribbon diagonally across top right and bottom left corners of layered rectangles, gluing ends on back. Adhere layered rectangle to card, centering rectangle over netting.

Transfer winter sentiment onto vellum; tear a 1½ x 3½-inch rectangle around word and apply blue ink to edges. Place vellum word over bottom right corner of photo; punch a hole on each end of the vellum and attach eyelets to holes. ■

SOURCES: Blue netting from Jest Charming Embellishments; rub-on transfer from Royal & Langnickel; Zip Dry paper adhesive from Beacon.

MATERIALS

White card stock
Clear vellum
Speckled blue netting
2 (3-inch) pieces ¼-inch-wide sheer iridescent ribbon
2 (⅛-inch) round white eyelets
Winter sentiment rub-on transfer
Light blue ink pad
Craft sponge
Instant-dry paper adhesive
Rotary tool and scoring blade
⅛-inch circle punch
Pinking shears
3 x 4½-inch horizontal winter photo

Warm Holiday Wishes

Design by BARBARA GREVE

Frame a photo with coordinating holiday papers to create a unique holiday greeting!

MATERIALS

5 x 6½-inch white note card
Ivory card stock
Clear vellum
Holly berry patterned paper
Rubber stamps: holly berries and holiday greeting
Black ink pad
Gold embossing powder
Clear embossing ink pad
Heat embossing tool
Metallic red cord
Instant-dry paper adhesive
Glue stick
Adhesive foam squares
Rotary cutter and scoring blade
Cutting mat
Desired photo

Cut a 5 x 6½-inch piece of holly berry patterned paper; adhere to front of card. Cut a 4⅝ x 3½-inch piece of ivory card stock; use black ink to stamp holly berries image over entire piece. Cut a 3 x 2-inch rectangle from center of stamped card stock.

Cut a ⅞ x 3⅞-inch piece of vellum; use the clear embossing ink to stamp the holiday greeting image onto vellum. Emboss with gold embossing powder. Apply embossing ink to the inside and outside edges of card-stock frame; emboss edges using gold embossing powder.

Attach adhesive squares to back of card-stock frame except for the top; adhere frame to card leaving room for holiday greeting. Use paper adhesive to attach holiday greeting below frame. Tie metallic cord into a bow and adhere to bottom of frame; trim ends. Cut photo to 2⅜ x 3¾ inches; slip into frame. ∎

SOURCES: Rubber stamps, ink pad and patterned paper from Anna Griffin; Zip Dry paper adhesive from Beacon.

Look What Santa Brought

Design courtesy of SHORTCUTS

Use a favorite photo to craft a holiday card embellished with metal hinges. Self-adhesive papers add texture!

Cut two pieces of textured cream card stock, one measuring 6 x 6½ inches and the other 4¼ x 5½ inches. Apply tan ink to edges of both pieces. Tear mulberry paper to fit onto larger piece of card stock; attach to card stock.

Using a computer and scanner, print desired photo onto aged cotton paper and adhere to smaller piece of card stock. Wrap ribbon around bottom and tie into a bow.

With a computer, print the following messages onto aged cotton: "Look What Santa Brought" for front of card and "Best Holiday Wishes from our Newest Addition" to be attached to inside of card. Cut each into a rectangle and adhere first message to the small piece of card stock; center and adhere second message to the larger piece of card stock.

To join card together, use eyelets to attach the hinges to the tops of both pieces. ∎

SOURCES: Mulberry paper and aged cotton from Shortcuts/Paramount Brands; hinges from Making Memories.

MATERIALS

Textured cream card stock
Self-adhesive burgundy
    mulberry paper
Self-adhesive aged cotton
    paper
Green gingham ribbon
2 metal scrapbook hinges
4 eyelets
Tan ink pad
Computer with scanner
Desired photo

Postage Stamp Magnets & Card

Designs by SHARON REINHART

Save your cropped photo scraps to create one-of-a-kind faux postage.
Back with magnets or attach to the front of a card for unique projects!

Magnets

Using gold ink, stamp small postage frame image twice onto light green card stock; apply gold embossing powder and emboss with heat tool. Cut out both images close to embossed lines. Cut photo into two pieces that both measure 1⅛ x 1⅜ inches. Adhere one to center of each of the embossed images. Adhere magnet to back of each piece.

Card

Cut a 5½ x 8½-inch piece of pink card stock; score and fold in half. Using gold ink, stamp large postage frame image onto light green card stock. Apply gold embossing powder and emboss with heat tool. Cut out image close to embossed lines. Cut photo into a 1⅞-inch square; adhere inside postage frame. Adhere frame image to left side of card using foam squares.

Punch two 1/16-inch holes ¼ inch apart below postage frame; cut a 3-inch piece of ribbon and insert ribbon through holes from front to back. Cross ribbons over and insert ribbon back through opposite holes to front; trim ends. ***Note:*** *Use a fine-tip stylus to help push ribbon back through holes.*

Stamp and emboss "Life is Sweet" sentiment onto a 1½ x 3¾-inch piece of green gingham-patterned paper. Layer piece onto a 2 x 4¼-inch piece of light green card stock using gold photo corners and double-sided tape. Adhere sentiment panel to right side of card. ∎

SOURCES: Rubber stamps from JudiKins and Hero Arts; patterned paper from K&Company.

Back of magnet.

MATERIALS

Light green and pink card stock
Green gingham-patterned paper
Rubber stamps: small postage frame, large postage frame and "Life is Sweet" sentiment
Gold pigment ink pad
Gold embossing powder
Embossing heat tool
4 gold photo corners
⅛-inch-wide light green satin ribbon
1/16-inch hole punch
Magnets
Glue stick
Adhesive foam squares
Double-sided tape
Bone folder
Fine-tip stylus
Flower photos

MATERIALS

- Papermaking kit
- Metallic dust, metallic sprinkles, mica chips and angel wings
- Card stock: light blue, green and yellow
- 3¾ x 4½-inch sheets of white paper
- Scrap paper
- Waxed paper
- Glass pebbles: blue, green and yellow
- 12 (⅛-inch) square gold eyelets
- ½ yard ¼-inch-wide satin ribbon: light blue, green and yellow
- Rubber stamps: decorative ribbon border and corner embellishment
- Gold pigment ink pad
- Instant-dry paper adhesive
- Bead adhesive
- Paintbrush
- ⅛- and ¼-inch circle punches
- Blender
- Iron
- Bone folder
- Rotary tool and scoring blade
- Fine sandpaper
- Black and white photos

Stamped Mini Books

Designs by MARY AYRES

Little books are just right for jotting down little thoughts and holding little photos!

Handmade Paper

Following manufacturer's instructions, use papermaking kit to create handmade paper. To make yellow paper, place torn pieces of yellow card stock and gold metallic dust in a blender. For blue paper, use torn pieces of blue card stock, blue angel wings and periwinkle mica chips. ***Note:*** *Remove seed pods from angel wings before using.* To make green paper, use torn pieces of green card stock, sage mica chips and metallic sprinkles. Place handmade papers between sheets of waxed paper; iron dry.

Stamped Mini Book

For the front and back covers, cut two 3¾ x 4½-inch rectangles from blue, green or yellow card stock. Score a line vertically on front cover ¾ inch from left side edge to create a binding.

Using gold ink, stamp decorative ribbon border image vertically on binding area of front cover. Stamp decorative corner image on the four corners of the front cover. ***Note:*** *Do not stamp corner image onto binding area.*

Apply gold ink to edges of front and back covers. Place a piece of scrap paper over binding, lining up edge with scored line and apply gold ink to left side of cover along edge of scrap paper.

Tear a 2-inch square from coordinating handmade paper; apply gold ink to edges and glue square in a diamond shape centered on the front cover.

Place coordinating glass pebble on chosen photo and cut around edges. Brush a thick layer of bead adhesive on back of pebble and adhere photo. Once dry, wipe sandpaper across edge of photo to sand edges even with pebble. Center and glue pebble to front cover.

Stack front and back covers together and punch two ⅛-inch holes in binding area ½ inch from top and bottom edges; attach eyelets. Punch ¼-inch holes in sheets of white paper (album pages) so they are lined up with cover holes. Stack album pages between covers. Insert coordinating ribbon through holes and tie into a bow. Trim bow ends; apply a small dot of glue under bow to secure. ∎

SOURCES: Papermaking kit, metallic dust, metallic sprinkles, mica chips and angel wings from Arnold Grummer; glass pebbles from JudiKins; rubber stamps from Plaid/All Night Media and Anna Griffin; Zip Dry and Gem-Tac adhesives from Beacon.

Abstract Photo Card

Design by JUDI KAUFFMAN

Make use of your "dud" photos by using the blurry images as a backdrop for rubber-stamp designs and motifs. Use these revamped images on cards, scrapbook pages or altered art!

MATERIALS

5 x 7-inch "dud" photo

8½ x 11-inch coordinating card stock

Tri-color opalescent ink pads in purple and pink hues

Large abstract rubber stamp

3 bottle caps

3 bottle-cap stickers

1½-inch-wide green sheer ribbon

Coordinating fibers

Adhesive foam squares

Craft glue

Instant-dry paper adhesive

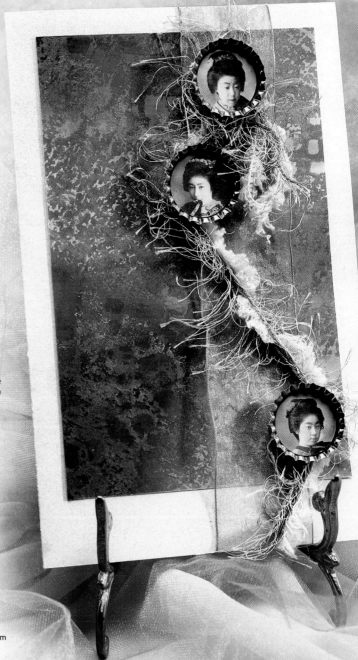

Use the purple hues tri-color ink pad to stamp abstract design over entire surface of "dud" photo; let dry. Repeat using the pink hues tri-color ink pad; let dry. Score and fold card stock in half; adhere stamped photo to card.

Place a sticker inside each bottle cap. Wrap a piece of green sheer ribbon around card front on right side; wrap and secure ends with glue inside card. Attach bottle caps to ribbon with adhesive foam squares. Glue fiber ends inside card and wrap fibers around bottle caps as desired; wrap several times around top cap and use a small dot of glue to secure. ∎

SOURCES: Rubber stamp from Red Castle, Inc.; bottle caps and bottle-cap stickers from Design Originals; Zip Dry and Kid's Choice glues from Beacon; Tsukineko Brilliance Tri-Color Ink Pads, Aurora & Twilight.

Designer & Project Listing

Paper Crafting Basics Paper crafting is easy, creative and fun. Collect basic tools and supplies, learn a few simple terms and techniques, and you're ready to start. The possibilities abound!

Cutting and Tearing

Craft knife, cutting mat Must-have tools. Mat protects work surface, keeps blades from getting dull.

Measure and mark Diagrams show solid lines for cutting, dotted lines for folding.

Other cutters Guillotine and rotary-blade paper cutters, oval and circle cutters, cutters that cut unusual shapes via a gear or cam system, swivel-blade knives that cut along the channels of plastic templates, and die cutting machines (large or small in size and price). Markers that draw as they cut.

Punches Available in hundreds of shapes and sizes ranging from $1/16$ inch to over 3 inches (use for eyelets, lettering, dimensional punch art, and embellishments). Also punches for two-ring, three-ring, coil, comb and disk binding.

Scissors Long and short blades that cut straight or a pattern. Scissors with nonstick coating are ideal for cutting adhesive sheets and tape, bonsai scissors best for cutting rubber or heavy board. Consider comfort—large holes for fingers, soft grips.

Tearing Tear paper for collage, special effects, layering on cards, scrapbook pages and more. Wet a small paintbrush; tear along the wet line for a deckle edge.

Embellishments

If you are not already a pack rat, it is time to start! Embellish projects with stickers, eyelets, brads, nail heads, wire, beads, iron-on ribbon and braid, memorabilia and printed ephemera.

Embossing

Dry embossing Use a light source, stencil, card stock and stylus tool. Add color, or leave raised areas plain.

Heat embossing Use embossing powder, ink, card stock and a heat tool to create raised designs and textures.

Powders come in a wide range of colors. Fine grain is called "detail" and heavier called "ultrathick." Embossing powders will not stick to most dye inks—use pigment inks or special clear embossing inks for best results.

Glues and Adhesives

Basics Each glue or adhesive is formulated for a particular use and specified surfaces. Read the label and carefully follow directions, especially those that involve personal safety and health.

Foam tape adds dimension.

Glue dots, adhesive sheets and cartridge type machines quick grab, no drying time needed.

Glue pens Fine line control.

Glue sticks Wide coverage.

Repositionable products Useful for stencils and temporary holding.

Measuring

Rulers A metal straightedge for cutting with a craft knife (a must-have tool). Match the length of the ruler to the project (shorter rulers are easier to use when working on smaller projects).

Quilter's grid ruler Use to measure squares and rectangles.

Pens and Markers

Choose inks (permanent, watercolor, metallic, etc.), **colors** (sold by sets or individually), **and nibs** (fine point, calligraphy, etc.) **to suit the project.** For journals and scrapbooks, make sure inks are permanent and fade-resistant.

Store pens and markers flat unless the manufacturer says otherwise.

Scoring and Folding

Folding Mountain folds—up, valley folds—down. Most patterns will have different types of dotted lines to denote mountain or valley folds.

Tools Scoring tool and bone folder. Fingernails will scar the surface of the paper.

Paper and Card Stock

Card stock Heavier and stiffer than paper. A sturdy surface for cards, boxes, ornaments.

Paper Lighter-weight surfaces used for drawing, stamping, collage.

Storage and organization Store paper flat and away from moisture.

Arrange by color, size or type. Keep your scraps for collage projects.

Types Handmade, milled, marbled, mulberry, origami, embossed, glossy, matte, botanical inclusions, vellum, parchment, preprinted, tissue and more.

Stamping

Direct-to-paper (DTP) Use ink pad, sponge or stylus tool to apply ink instead of a rubber stamp.

Inks Available in pads and re-inker bottles. Types include dye and pigment, permanent, waterproof and fade-resistant or archival, chalk-finish, fast-drying, slow-drying, rainbow and more. Read the labels to determine what is best for a project or surface.

Make stamps Carve rubber, erasers, carving blocks, vegetables. Heat Magic Stamp foam blocks to press against textures. Stamp found objects such as leaves and flowers, keys and coins, etc.

Stamps Sold mounted on wood, acrylic or foam, or unmounted (rubber part only), made from vulcanized rubber, acrylic or foam.

Store Flat and away from light and heat.

Techniques Tap the ink onto the stamp (using the pad as the applicator) or tap the stamp onto the ink pad. Stamp with even hand pressure (no rocking) for best results. For very large stamps, apply ink with a brayer. Color the surface of a stamp with watercolor markers (several colors), huff with breath to keep the colors moist, then stamp; or lightly spray with water mist before stamping for a very different effect.

Unmounted stamps Mount temporarily on acrylic blocks with Scotch Poster Tape on one surface (nothing on the rubber stamp) or one of the other methods (hook and loop, paint on adhesives, cling plastic).

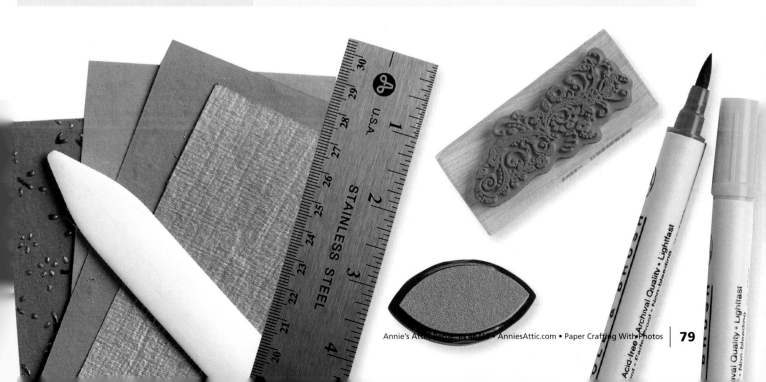

Buyer's Guide

3M, Consumer Stationery Division, P.O. Box 33594, St. Paul, MN 55133

7 Gypsies, (800) 588-6707, www.7gypsies.com

Anna Griffin Inc., 733 Lambert Dr., Atlanta, GA 30324, www.annagriffin.com

Arnold Grummer (Greg Markim), www.arnoldgrummer.com

Artifacts Inc., www.artifactsinc.com

Bazzill Basics, 701 N. Golden Key St., Gilbert, AZ 85233

Beacon Adhesives Inc., 125 MacQuestan Pkwy. S., Mount Vernon, NY 10550, (914) 699-3400

Biblical Impressions, (877) 587-0941, www.biblical.com

Brandess-Kalt-Aetna Group Inc., 701 Corporate Woods Pkwy., Vernon Hills, IL 60061, (847) 821-0450

Clearsnap Inc., P.O. Box 98, Anacortes, WA 98221-0098, (360) 293-6634, www.clearsnap.com

Close to My Heart, 1199 W. 700 S., Pleasant Grove, UT 84062, www.closetomyheart.com

Creative Imaginations, (800) 942-6487, www.cigift.com

Creative Impressions, 2520 W. Colorado Ave., Colorado Springs, CO 80904, (719) 596-4860

Delta/Rubber Stampede, (800) 423-4135, www.deltacrafts.com

DeNami Design, www.denamidesign.com

Design Originals, www.d-originals.com

Duncan Enterprises, 5673 E. Shields Ave., Fresno, CA 93727, (800) 438-6226

Dymo, www.dymo.com

EK Success Ltd., 125 Entin Rd., Clifton, NJ 07014

Emagination Crafts, 463 W. Wrightwood Ave., Elmhurst, IL 60126

Fibers by the Yard, 2818 Devonshire Dr., Norman, OK 73071, (405) 364-8066

Fiskars, 7811 W. Stewart Ave., Wausau, WI 54401-8027

FoofaLa, www.foofala.com

Glue Dots International, www.gluedots.com

Golden Artist Colors Inc., 188 Bell Rd., New Berlin, NY 13411-9527, (800) 959-6543

Hero Arts Rubber Stamps, 1343 Powell St., Emeryville, CA 94608

Jest Charming Embellishments, www.jestcharming.com

JudiKins, www.judikins.com

K&Company, 8500 N.W. River Park Dr., Pillar #136, Parkville, MO 64152

KI Memories, www.kimemories.com

Krylon/Sherwin-Williams Co., Craft Customer Service, W. 101 Prospect Ave., Cleveland, OH 44115

Lasting Impressions for Paper Inc., 2441 S. 1560 W. Woods Cross, UT 84087, (800) 9-EMBOSS

Lazertran, www.lazertran.com, (800) 245-7547

Magenta Rubber Stamps, www.magentarubberstamps.com

Making Memories, 1168 W. 500 N., Centerville, UT 84014, (801) 294-0430

Me & My Big Ideas, 20321 Valencia Circle, Lake Forest, CA 92630

MPR Associates Inc., P.O. Box 7343, 529 Townsend Ave., High Point, NC 27264-7343, (800) 334-1047

Neato Stuff, P.O. Box 4466, Carson City, NV 89702

Paper Mart, www.papermart.com

Pebbles Inc., www.pebblesinc.com

Plaid/All Night Media, 3225 Westech Dr., Norcross, GA 30092

Provo Craft/Sizzix, mail-order source: **Creative Express,** 295 W. Center St., Provo, UT 84601-4436

Red Castle Inc., www.redcastle.com

River City Rubber Works, 5555 S. Meridian, Wichita, KS 67217, (877) 735-2276

Royal & Langnickel, www.royalbrush.com

Sandylion, P.O. Box 1570, Buffalo, NY 14240-1570, www.sandylion.com

Shortcuts/Paramount Brands, 3950 Paramount Blvd., Suite 100, Lakewood, CA 90712, (866) 329-9800

Stampendous, 1240 N. Red Gum, Anaheim, CA 92806-1820, (800) 869-0474

Stampin' Up!, (800)STAMPUP, www.stampinup.com

Stampola, www.stampola.com

Stewart Superior, www.stewartsuperior.com

Sulyn Industries Inc., 11927 W. Sample Rd., Coral Springs, FL 33065

Therm O Web, 770 Glenn Ave., Wheeling, IL 60090, (847) 520-5200

Tsukineko Inc., 17640 N.E. 65th St., Redmond, WA 98052, (800) 769-6633, www.tsukineko.com

USArtQuest Inc., 7800 Ann Arbor Rd., Grass Lake, MI 49240, (517) 522-6225, www.usartquest.com

Walnut Hollow, 1409 State Road 23, Dodgeville, WI 53533, (800) 950-5101, www.walnuthollow.com

Xyron, 15820 N. 84th St., Scottsdale, AZ 85260, (800) 793-3523

The Buyer's Guide listings are provided as a service to our readers and should not be considered an endorsement from this publication.